ORINDA

P9-DVQ-267

WITHDRAWN

THIS BOOK IS A GIFT OF:
FRIENDS OF THE ORINDA LIBRARY

CONTRA COSTA COUNTY LIBRARY

THE LOOK-IT-UP BOOK OF

Explorers

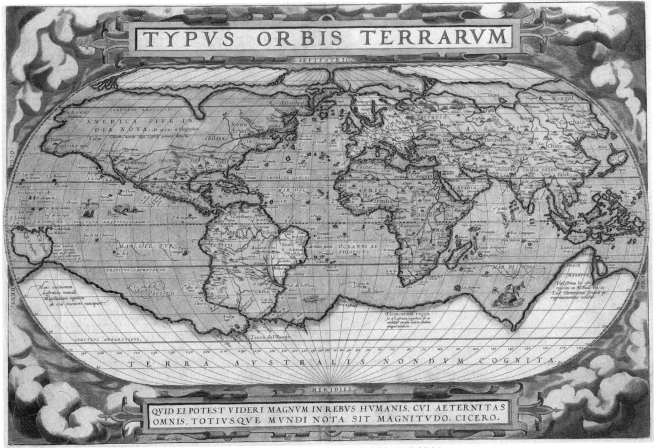

TYPVS ORBIS TERRARVM

QVID EI POTEST VIDERI MAGNVM IN REBVS HVMANIS, CVI AETERNITAS
OMNIS, TOTIVSQVE MVNDI NOTA SIT MAGNITVDO. CICERO.

CONTRA COSTA COUNTY LIBRARY

Elizabeth Cody Kimmel

Random House 🏠 New York

3 1901 03748 4583

For my daughter, Emma Cody Kimmel, whose heart spans the oceans and whose mind reaches for the stars —*E.C.K.*

The author and editors would like to thank Peter C. Mancall, Professor of History, University of Southern California, for his help in the preparation of this book.

Photographs: © Glen Allison/Photodisc/PictureQuest, pp. 28, 60; © Bettmann/CORBIS, pp. 9, 18, 72, 92, 103, 118, 119, 121, 124; courtesy of www.canadianheritage.ca, National Archives of Canada, pp. 16 (top), 35; courtesy of City of New Bedford Office of Tourism and Marketing, p. 44; © Philippe Colombi/Photodisc/PictureQuest, p. 69; © CORBIS, pp. 58, 82 (top); © Adam Crowley/Photodisc/ PictureQuest, p. 73; © Digital Vision Ltd., pp. 1, 5, 15, cover (background); © Geostock/Photodisc/PictureQuest, p. 30 (bottom); © Jeff Haynes/AFP/Getty Images, p. 86; © Hulton Archive/Getty Images, pp. 52, 88; © Hulton-Deutsch Collection/CORBIS, pp. 104 (top), 106; courtesy Independence National Historical Park, p. 40 (top and bottom); © Jacques Langevin/CORBIS SYGMA, p. 70; © Charles & Josette Lenars/CORBIS, p. 25; Library of Congress, Prints and Photographs Division, pp. 24, 27, 30 (top), 38, 43, 46 (top and bottom), 48, 51, 55, 61, 64, 66, 78, 80, 85, 91, 94 (top and bottom), 95, 125; © Map Resources, pp. 6–7; © The Mariners' Museum, pp. 12, 13, 16 (bottom), 21; courtesy of NASA, pp. 109, 110, 112, 113, 115, 116; by permission of the National Library of Australia, pp. 76, 82 (bottom); courtesy of the National Library of Canada, pp. 33, 35, 36, 79, 89, 97, 101; courtesy of Parks Canada/J. Steeves, p. 10; © PhotoLink/Photodisc/PictureQuest, pp. 54, 75, 100, 104 (bottom); © Reuters NewMedia Inc./CORBIS, p. 107; © Joel W. Rogers/COR- BIS, cover (foreground); © Adalberto Rios Szalay/Sexto Sol/Photodisc/PictureQuest, p. 83; © John Wang/Photodisc/PictureQuest, p. 63; © Kennan Ward/CORBIS, p. 49; © Ralph White/CORBIS, p. 122; © Michael S. Yamashita/CORBIS, p. 57.

Text copyright © 2004 by Elizabeth Cody Kimmel.
Maps copyright © 2004 by Bryn Barnard.
All rights reserved under International and Pan-American Copyright Conventions. Published in the United States by Random House Children's Books, a division of Random House, Inc., New York, and simultaneously in Canada by Random House of Canada Limited, Toronto.

www.randomhouse.com/kids

Library of Congress Cataloging-in-Publication Data
Kimmel, Elizabeth Cody.
The look-it-up book of explorers / by Elizabeth Cody Kimmel ; illustrated by Bryn Barnard. — 1st ed.
p.   cm.
Includes index.
ISBN 0-375-82478-2 (trade) — ISBN 0-375-92478-7 (lib. bdg.)
1. Explorers—Biography—Juvenile literature. 2. Discoveries in geography—Juvenile literature.
I. Barnard, Bryn, ill. II. Title.
G200.K56 2004 910'.92'2—dc22   2004002922

Printed in the United States of America

First Edition   10 9 8 7 6 5 4 3 2 1

RANDOM HOUSE and colophon are registered trademarks of Random House, Inc.

Contents

Timeline

c. 983
Erik the Red discovers Greenland.

1000
Leif Eriksson lands on the North American continent.

1271–1295
Marco Polo travels throughout Asia.

1325
Ibn Battuta leaves on his pilgrimage to Mecca.

1405
Zheng He embarks on the first of seven voyages to over thirty countries.

1424–1458
Prince Henry the Navigator sends forth voyages of discovery to Africa's western coast.

1488
Bartolomeu Dias rounds Africa's southernmost tip, the Cape of Good Hope.

1492
Christopher Columbus lands on the island of San Salvador, ushering in a period of unprecedented exploration of the Americas.

1494
The Treaty of Tordesillas establishes an imaginary line of demarcation around the globe.

1497
John Cabot claims North America for England.

1498
Vasco da Gama becomes the first known European to reach India by sea.

1519
Hernán Cortés explores Mexico, eventually destroying the Aztec civilization.

1520
Ferdinand Magellan finds the Strait of Magellan. His expedition circumnavigates the world.

1532
Francisco Pizarro captures the Inca leader, Atahuallpa.

1534–1535
Jacques Cartier discovers Prince Edward Island and the St. Lawrence River.

1580
Sir Francis Drake becomes the second explorer to circumnavigate the world.

1585
Sir Walter Raleigh brings the first colonists to Roanoke Island.

1608
Samuel de Champlain establishes the first permanent French settlement in Canada.

1609
Henry Hudson explores the Hudson River as far north as Albany.

1642
Abel Janszoon Tasman discovers Van Diemen's Land (later named Tasmania).

1648
Semen Dezhnev discovers the Bering Strait, which separates Asia and North America.

1728
Vitus Bering rediscovers and names the Bering Strait.

1775
Daniel Boone clears the Wilderness Road to Kentucky.

1778
James Cook explores the Hawaiian islands.

1787
Jean-François de Galaup, Comte de la Pérouse charts Asian coastlines for France.

1795–1796
Mungo Park explores Africa's Niger River.

1803
Matthew Flinders circumnavigates Australia.

1805
Lewis and Clark explore the North American continent all the way to the Pacific Ocean.

1819
Sir William Edward Parry leads the first overwinter expedition in the Arctic.

1839–1843
Sir James Clark Ross explores the Ross Sea and other key Antarctic areas.

1845
Sir John Franklin disappears looking for the Northwest Passage.

1858
Sir Richard Burton and *John Hanning Speke* discover Lake Tanganyika in Africa.

1871
Sir Henry Morton Stanley finds the missing *Dr. David Livingstone* in Africa's interior.

1893
Fridtjof Nansen allows his ship, the *Fram*, to freeze into the Arctic pack ice and be carried toward the North Pole.

1897
Mary Kingsley publishes her book *Travels in West Africa*.

1905
Roald Amundsen finds the Northwest Passage.

1908
Sir Ernest Shackleton makes the first ascent of Mount Erebus and comes within one hundred miles of the South Pole.

1908
Frederick Cook claims to reach the North Pole.

1909
Robert Edwin Peary and *Matthew Henson* claim to reach the North Pole.

1911
Roald Amundsen reaches the South Pole.

1912
Robert Falcon Scott dies returning from South Pole.

1924
Alexandra David-Néel becomes the first European woman to visit the forbidden holy city of Lhasa.

1931
Auguste Piccard becomes the first person to reach the stratosphere.

1934
William Beebe descends 3,028 feet into the ocean in the bathysphere.

1942
Jacques Cousteau develops the portable Aqua-Lung (now called scuba).

1953
Sir Edmund Hillary summits Mount Everest.

1957–1958
Sir Vivian Fuchs crosses Antarctica, mapping never-before-seen parts of the interior.

1960
Jacques Piccard and U.S. Navy Lieutenant *Donald Walsh* descend to the bottom of the Marianas Trench, 6.78 miles under the sea.

1961
Yuri Gagarin becomes the first person to reach outer space.

1962
John Glenn orbits the earth for the United States.

1963
Valentina Tereshkova becomes the first woman to travel in space.

1969
Neil Armstrong is the first person to stand on the moon's surface.

1983
Sally Ride becomes the first American woman to orbit the earth.

1985
Robert Ballard discovers the wreck of the *Titanic*.

ORNANDO VTRIQVE DICANTVR

The dictionary defines the word *explore* as "to travel over new territory for adventure or discovery." Since the time of the earliest recorded human history, we have evidence that humans have expressed and acted on their unquenchable desire to venture into the unknown. The reasons behind expeditions of exploration were often economic or political, most easily summarized as the simple desire for more wealth and more land. However, the individuals who carried out these expeditions also shared traits of courage, curiosity, restlessness, ambition, and the willingness to undergo the most severe hardships in the name of discovery.

The scope and arena of exploration have changed drastically since the time of the ancient Egyptians, when the earliest known recorded expeditions occurred. Centuries ago, expeditions crossed oceans to search for new continents. Today no areas of *terra incognita,* or unknown lands, remain. But the human drive to extend the frontier of knowledge continues to push us in new directions, from the depths of the ocean to the rocky landscape of Mars. As long as humankind remains committed to adventure and discovery, there will be new frontiers to reach. The story of exploration remains a work in progress.

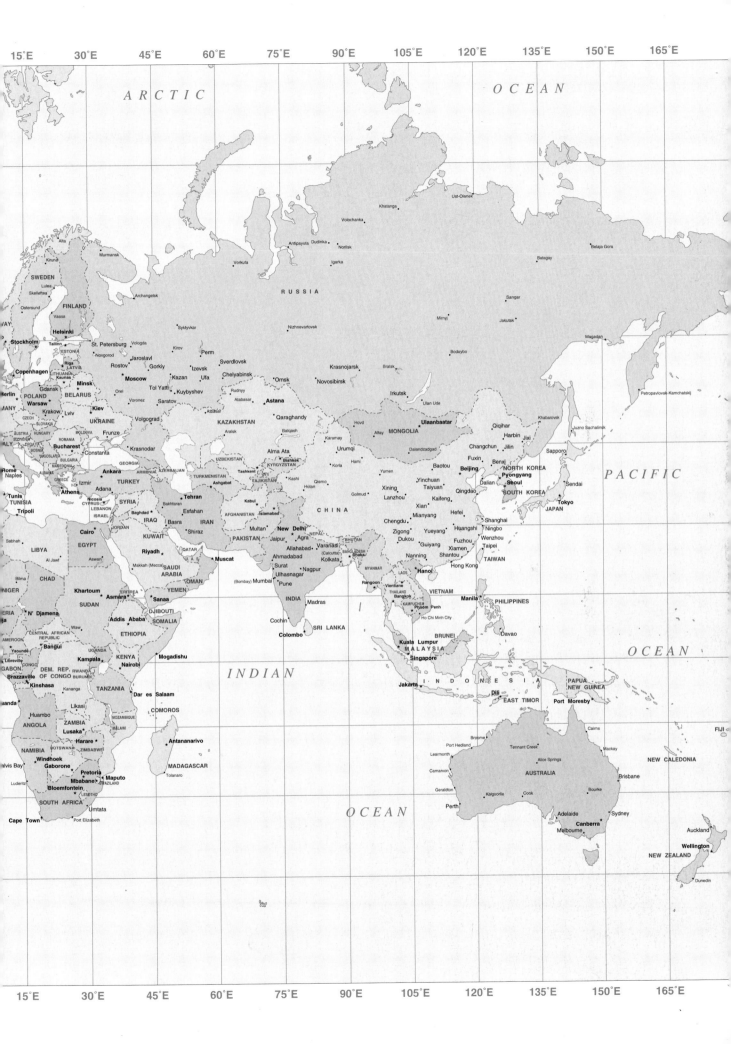

Leif Eriksson

born c. 978

Almost five hundred years before Christopher Columbus embarked on his historic journey in search of the New World, a sleek Viking boat crossed the Atlantic and arrived on the shores of North America. The expedition's leader was a young man named Leif Eriksson. He is the first European known to have visited and explored part of North America.

In Leif Eriksson's time, Viking history was not written but instead was passed down orally from generation to generation. It took over two hundred years for his story to be recorded, in what we now call *The Greenlanders' Saga*. As with any story passed down over centuries, it is difficult to know what details have changed or been left out. But *The Greenlanders' Saga* is the primary source of information about the Viking expeditions across the Atlantic in Leif's time.

Leif Eriksson was born in Iceland sometime around the year AD 978. He was the son of Erik the Red, a Norwegian who immigrated to Iceland. The days of the legendary Viking raids of plunder and terror were coming to a close. The Vikings were also herders and farmers, and they became increasingly reliant on this way of life. As Norway's population

grew, the Vikings needed more farmland to grow food. Leading the quest to find new land, Erik discovered and explored an island to the west. He established a colony of Icelandic settlers there and called it Greenland. It was here that his son Leif first heard stories of land sighted even farther west.

When Leif was able to obtain a longboat of his own, he organized a westbound expedition. He provisioned his square-sailed longboat with food, weapons, tools, and thirty-five adventuresome Norse Greenlanders. With the blessing of his father, who was unable to accompany him due to an injury, Leif Eriksson sailed west from Greenland into largely unknown waters. The year was AD 1000.

Leif had only a vague expectation of what he might find, based on land sightings made by a trader named Bjarni Herjolfsson around the year 986. Lost in fog, the trader had sailed blindly until he came to a hilly coast covered with trees. Correcting his course and heading back east toward Iceland, the trader had twice more glimpsed land but kept sailing.

Leif and his men saw land twice in the first week or ten days on the sea. Both times they briefly went ashore. Leif named the first place Helluland, which meant the Land of Flat Stones. The second place Leif called Markland, meaning the Land of Forests. But Leif was determined to reach the third place Bjarni had described, the coastline of hills

and old trees. After several more days, the sailors found it.

Off the coast lay a grassy island, which they briefly explored before sailing to an inlet close to shore. Here was the land Leif had hoped to find. It was thick with large trees, which could provide valuable timber for treeless Greenland. A river gave access to fresh water and fish. Leif decided to build a camp and spend the winter exploring. The months that Leif spent in the new land confirmed his feeling that it was a country rich with resources. In addition to the timber and fish,

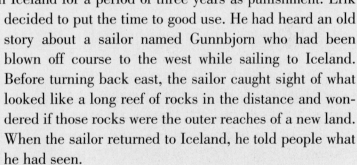

Erik the Red

Erik the Red, father of Leif Eriksson, is important enough in Viking history to have a saga named after him: *Erik the Red's Saga*. With *The Greenlanders' Saga*, it constitutes *The Vinland Saga*. These sagas were the result of hundreds of years of oral history finally written down in Iceland at the beginning of the thirteenth century.

The saga relates that Erik the Red was found guilty of killing two men. The court ruled that Erik be banished from his home and family in Iceland for a period of three years as punishment. Erik

decided to put the time to good use. He had heard an old story about a sailor named Gunnbjorn who had been blown off course to the west while sailing to Iceland. Before turning back east, the sailor caught sight of what looked like a long reef of rocks in the distance and wondered if those rocks were the outer reaches of a new land. When the sailor returned to Iceland, he told people what he had seen.

Erik believed that the Gunnbjorn Skerries, as they were called, did exist and really were the gateway to an undiscovered country. During his banishment, he and his servants took a longboat and headed west, probably in the year 983. He found what he sought, and the new land later became known as Greenland. Erik returned to Iceland after his banishment and organized a group of colonists, including his family, to live and farm on the new land. Erik the Red's western settlement began the long history of the Norse people on Greenland.

there was plenty of game for hunting. Due to the abundance of wild grapes, Leif named the country Vinland.

Throughout the summer, small parties headed south to explore. They caught enough wild game and salmon to keep all of the men well fed. Leif and his party stayed all winter at their camp in Vinland. When spring came, he readied his group and their longboat for the journey home. Leif's return to his family was triumphant—he had found what he had sought. His accomplishments were great enough to be included in the Vikings' oral histories, eventually written down in *The Greenlanders' Saga* in the thirteenth century. The sagas go on to tell of further adventures in North America by Leif's brother and sister

and a man named Thorfin Karlsefni, who intended to start a permanent settlement. The Vikings eventually abandoned all settlements in Vinland, possibly after clashes with Native Americans.

Recent discoveries in Newfoundland have proved that the legends in *The Greenlanders' Saga* about Leif Eriksson are true. In the 1960s, archaeologists excavated a Viking settlement at L'Anse aux Meadows dating from almost exactly the time Leif Eriksson was said to have been there. Though these settlements were eventually abandoned, it is now accepted that Leif Eriksson landed on the continent of North America some five hundred years before the more widely known explorer Christopher Columbus.

Leif's Camp

The camp was a series of eight buildings, each built over a frame of timber filled in with sod and smaller branches. Three large houses each contained a large room surrounded by several small rooms. The houses, built in the style of the Icelandic structures Leif had known as a boy, contained living quarters, a workshop, a kitchen area, and a storage room. By each house was a smaller hut that could provide additional work and storage space. The group of buildings was meant to serve not just as their winter quarters but also as a base for future Viking expeditions.

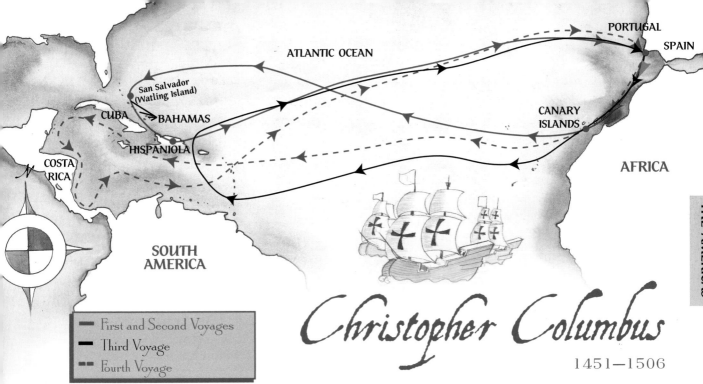

Christopher Columbus
1451–1506

On September 6, 1492, a group of three sailing ships departed from the Canary Islands off the coast of northern Africa. The names of the ships would one day be known by schoolchildren everywhere. For the moment, the <u>Niña</u>, the <u>Pinta</u>, and the <u>Santa María</u> were as unknown as the expedition leader himself, Christopher Columbus. The ships had sailed south along the coast of Africa from Spain. At the Canary Islands, Columbus planned to turn west to the open sea, leaving all known and mapped land behind him. To Columbus's knowledge, he was the first to sail these waters. He felt certain that once he crossed them, he would find Asia, and along with it the fabled land of Cipangu, which today we call Japan. Such a discovery, with the potential of unimaginable wealth and glory for Spain, would surely be one of the greatest achievements of exploration in history.

Born in 1451 in the Italian city of Genoa, Columbus belonged to a family of weavers of modest means. In all likelihood, young Columbus learned wool weaving from his father. He also took his first sea voyage while still relatively young. Genoa was a port city, and there were plenty of opportunities for a young man to sign on as a messenger or sailor. He was largely self-educated, and some scholars believe that the report that Columbus attended the University of Pavia is untrue. What is known is that Columbus was a man of huge ambition, both socially and materially. He wished to obtain power and wealth and to move in the social circles of nobility. He also had boundless curiosity.

As a young man, Columbus moved to the Portuguese city of Lisbon. He was keenly interested in navigation, exploration, and adventure, and here he found many men of like mind. His aspirations were born through his discussions and reading, including the ideas of Ptolemy and the writings of Marco Polo. Polo's descriptions of the fabled island of Cipangu (Japan) seized Columbus's imagination. He was convinced that the continent of Asia, and Cipangu, lay less than three thousand miles west across the Atlantic Ocean. Columbus became obsessed with the idea of heading an expedition to establish this transoceanic route to Asia. To do so, he would have to find a wealthy patron willing to pay for the ships and supplies he needed. His efforts to secure a sponsor failed in Italy, England, and Portugal. After years of trying, he finally met with Ferdinand and Isabella, king and queen of Spain. Convinced that Columbus could find Cipangu, the monarchs agreed to support his journey. They expected him to claim land and gold in the name of Spain.

Christopher Columbus kneels before King Ferdinand and Queen Isabella of Spain.

Columbus hastily manned and provisioned the *Niña,* the *Pinta,* and his own ship, the *Santa María.* In September 1492, they sailed down the coast of Africa to the Canary Islands. Here Columbus turned his ships west into the heart of the Atlantic Ocean, away from every known and charted landfall.

The sailors became more uneasy with each passing day. They were unaccustomed to being in the middle of the ocean with no promise of land nearby. Finally on Friday, October 12, 1492, a Sevillian sailor on duty aloft gave the cry of *"Tierra!"* After over a month sailing in unknown seas, the crew was relieved to see land. No one was more excited than Columbus. He believed he had landed on an island off the coast of Asia, within sailing distance of Cipangu. In reality, Columbus was on an island in the outer Bahamas, some 250 miles northeast of Cuba.

Though the island was populated and known by its people as Guanahani, Columbus called the island San Salvador, meaning "Holy Savior." With the disregard for native inhabitants common to explorers of his day, Columbus took possession of the land in the name of Spain. Neither the native nor the Spanish name has survived— today the island is known as Watling Island, though it is still called San Salvador by some.

Columbus explored San Salvador and the nearby islands for three months, always hoping to find Cipangu and its mountains of gold. Though the natives were largely friendly and helpful, Columbus managed to find only a very small amount of gold. Still, he was convinced that the continent of Asia lay nearby and that this would be a highly advantageous place to begin a colony.

When the *Santa María* was damaged by rocks near the island of Hispaniola (present-day Haiti and the Dominican Republic),

Engraving of Christopher Columbus

Columbus transferred himself and his belongings to the *Niña*. From the *Santa María*'s wreckage, a fort was built at La Navidad, and forty-three men were left there to begin the colony and continue searching for gold while Columbus returned to Spain.

Columbus crossed the ocean to Portugal and then continued home to Spain in the *Niña*. By all accounts, his return was a triumph, and rewards and honors were heaped upon him by the king and queen. But Columbus still had to prove he had done what he set out to do. He was unswerving in his belief that the islands he had reached and begun to colonize were off the coast of Asia and that somewhere Cipangu lay among them.

Between 1493 and his death in 1506, Columbus made three additional trips to the islands, further colonizing Hispaniola and continuing to search for a passage to the mainland. His experiences ranged from disappointing to disastrous. On his second voyage, he found the settlement he had left behind in Hispaniola was in ruins—during his absence natives had killed every one of his men. He established a new colony in its

place, but its men were difficult to discipline and uncooperative with the natives. Columbus authorized the use of forced native labor to mine the gold he needed to bring back to Spain, but his command was disintegrating. By the time he returned to Spain from his second trip, a commissioner had been appointed to judge Columbus's ability to rule.

The questions were resolved enough to enable Columbus to return to his new world for a third time. On this trip, while further exploring islands to the south of Hispaniola, he caught sight of continental South America for the first time. Seemingly always destined to mistake one landmass for another, Columbus named his finding the Island of Zeta. At this time, Queen Isabella learned that Columbus's colonists on Hispaniola were staging a full revolt, one half against the other. Columbus admitted he could not bring the colonists to a peaceful resolution. The queen sent a judge to the colony to evaluate the situation, and he responded by putting Columbus in chains and returning him to Spain.

Once again, the questions about Columbus's conduct were resolved sufficiently to avoid further legal procedures. Amazingly, the Spanish king and queen agreed to send Columbus on yet another voyage to the New World, though he had to promise to avoid the colony on Hispaniola. The purpose of this voyage was primarily the gathering of precious metals, stones, and spices. He sailed along the coast of present-day Costa Rica, but his voyage was so beset by bad luck and slowed by an unwilling crew that he returned to Seville.

When he died two years later, he was disillusioned, his dreams unfulfilled. Yet Christopher Columbus had gone from a cloth maker of modest means to a man called admiral, governor, and counsellor to the king. Though he never went near Asia or Japan, his name will never be forgotten.

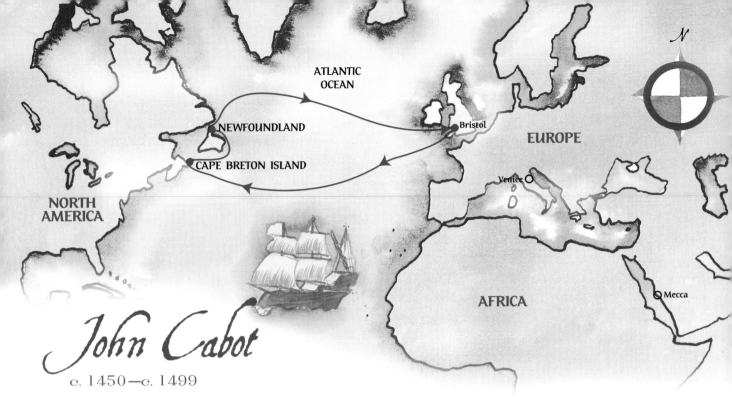

John Cabot

c. 1450–c. 1499

Of all the explorers who made a name for themselves in the Age of Discovery, perhaps the most mysterious is John Cabot. Though in his own lifetime Cabot was widely recognized and rewarded in England, the most basic information about his life is based only on guesswork. Depending on the source, Cabot was either instrumental in establishing a British claim on North America and opening valuable trade opportunities across the Atlantic or his claims were falsified by others eager to take credit for a continental landing. Over five hundred years after Cabot's death, new facts are still coming to light. The most convincing evidence that Cabot did what he claimed was not discovered until the 1950s, in a document now called the <u>John Day Letter</u>.

Cabot was probably born in present-day Italy around 1450. He worked as a merchant in the spice trade in Venice as a young man and gained experience in sailing trips that took him as far as Mecca, on the Arabian Peninsula. His experiences in the profitable world of trading Asian goods probably inspired his vision of discovering a faster and more efficient sea route to the Indies.

Cabot ultimately settled in Bristol, England, with his wife and children. He approached King Henry VII, looking for royal support for a proposed journey to China by sailing northwest across the Atlantic Ocean.

The king, who regretted turning down a similar proposal from a man named Columbus, agreed to be Cabot's patron and provide royal and financial support for the journey.

The discovery of a northwest passage to the Orient would provide huge opportunities in trade and riches to the country that discovered it. With his sailing experience and passion for Asia, Cabot was most likely familiar with the details and route of Christopher Columbus's journeys across the Atlantic. Cabot felt that by keeping significantly farther north on his voyage, he would discover a faster and more direct route to the New

World. Like Columbus, Cabot believed that the land across the Atlantic was Asia.

Cabot also had the backing of the merchants of Bristol. A busy port with a thriving shipbuilding industry, Bristol was the starting point for many Atlantic voyages. The city's merchants prized Asian spices and silks. Such goods were in high demand and very costly to obtain. If Cabot was right and he really did discover a shortcut to China, the merchants who backed him would stand to win an enormous profit and trade advantage.

Cabot sailed from Bristol in his small ship, the *Matthew,* in May 1497. His crew numbered only about twenty men, less than a quarter the size of Columbus's crews for his 1492 expedition. Cabot's party landed in the northern reaches of North America, coming ashore somewhere in present-day Newfoundland or Cape Breton Island, Canada. However, still believing, as many did, that Columbus had reached Asia, Cabot thought that he had landed in the vicinity of China.

By officially taking possession of this new land in the name of King Henry VII, John Cabot secured his place in history books. His was the first English claim to the territory of North America. Conflicting claims by different countries would continue for hundreds of years.

Many of the details of Cabot's expedition are contained in a letter from a man named John Day, believed to have been written to Christopher Columbus in 1498. The letter

The Sea Serpent

*M*en such as those on Cabot's 1497 voyage to the New World were for the most part seasoned sailors. There was little they had not seen or experienced. But the sea breeds legends, and one of the most enduring is that of sea serpents or sea monsters. Sailing into the unknown, the men might well have feared encountering many different kinds of beasts. Vicious sea monsters were said to crush the life out of ships by wrapping their serpentine bodies around ships' hulls. Then they would pick up the helpless sailors in their gigantic teeth.

These stories about sea monsters were probably based on glimpses of a very real species—*Architeuthis,* or the giant squid, which is thought to grow to sixty feet in length and weigh over a ton. Its giant, dinner-plate-size eyes are the largest in the entire animal kingdom. Its eight arms are covered with powerful, toothed suckers. Between two additional feeding tentacles, the giant squid has a sharp beak. Reports of the giant squid date back to ancient times, but no record exists of verified sightings until the mid-nineteenth century. It was not until recently that science even accepted the giant squid as something more than a type of Loch Ness monster fable.

Even today, after many exhaustive searches, no live, healthy giant squid has ever been observed or filmed in its home in the deepest waters of the ocean. It is no wonder that this mysterious and terrifying creature has inspired monstrous legends among seafarers for centuries.

confirms that Cabot landed in a country of towering trees. Exploration of the area suggested people were living there, though none were seen. Several other letters and a map drawn in 1500 by Juan de la Cosa also appear to confirm that Cabot landed on the North American continent and returned to England with new and accurate information about the coastline. King Henry VII granted him a cash award and an annual pension for his accomplishments.

The details of John Cabot's death are based only on theories. It is widely believed that Cabot embarked on a second voyage to the New World in 1498 and was never heard from again. Some evidence suggests Cabot reached North America and was killed there, either by Native Americans or Spanish explorers. Though Cabot remains to this day one of England's most famous explorers, the truth about his life and death may never be known.

Profile of John Cabot engraved on a commemorative medallion

Sebastian Cabot

Was Sebastian Cabot a trailblazing explorer or a calculating hoaxster? True to the murky history of his father, John, Sebastian Cabot left more questions than answers about his life.

Because of the wording of the patent originally granted to John Cabot by King Henry VII, we know that Sebastian and his two brothers were included in the royal authorization for John Cabot's 1497 voyage on the *Matthew*. We don't know whether Sebastian Cabot actually accompanied his father on that journey. Sebastian Cabot's written accounts describe himself as the joint discoverer of North America, along with his father. For many years, whether through his own efforts or misunderstanding, Sebastian Cabot was given the primary credit for his father's most outstanding accomplishments.

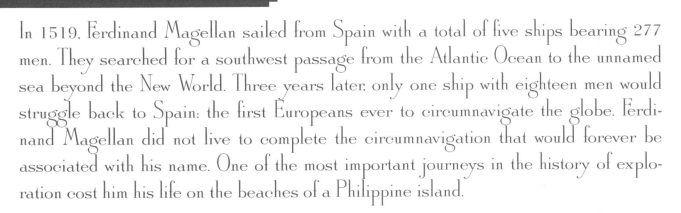

NORTH AMERICA

PORTUGAL

SPAIN

ATLANTIC OCEAN

ASIA

AFRICA

PHILIPPINES

GUAM

PACIFIC OCEAN

SOUTH AMERICA

BRAZIL

Line of Demarcation 1494

Moluccas (Spice Islands)

AUSTRALIA

PATAGONIA (ARGENTINA)

N

ATLANTIC OCEAN

Creek of Sardines

PACIFIC OCEAN

― Route of the *Victoria*
■ Strait of Magellan

Ferdinand Magellan

c. 1480—1521

In 1519, Ferdinand Magellan sailed from Spain with a total of five ships bearing 277 men. They searched for a southwest passage from the Atlantic Ocean to the unnamed sea beyond the New World. Three years later, only one ship with eighteen men would struggle back to Spain: the first Europeans ever to circumnavigate the globe. Ferdinand Magellan did not live to complete the circumnavigation that would forever be associated with his name. One of the most important journeys in the history of exploration cost him his life on the beaches of a Philippine island.

Though his final voyage saw him in the service of the Spanish, Ferdinand Magellan was of noble Portuguese birth. He spent many years serving in a Portuguese fleet, seeing battle several times. One such battle left him with a permanent limp. For reasons that may never be quite clear, Portugal's King Manuel disliked Magellan. Given his years of service to the Crown and conquest with the Portuguese fleet, Magellan might well have expected that his request for a promotion would be granted. But King Manuel flatly turned him down and stated that the Crown had no further use for the mariner. Stunned and humiliated, Magellan decided to offer his services to Portugal's greatest rival: Spain.

Magellan presented his plan to Spain's King Charles I (who later became Emperor Charles V). It had been over twenty years since Columbus made his first voyage to the New World. It was now generally accepted that the continent containing the New World stood between the eastern and western oceans. Since the circumference of the world was unknown, it was impossible to calculate east-west distances with any accuracy. But with the help of a local astrologer, Magellan calculated that he could locate a passage through the New World linking the two oceans and that once through he could reach the Spice Islands by this western ocean route.

Any trade route to the riches of the Moluccas, or Spice Islands, was a prize eagerly sought by fiercely competitive Spain and Portugal. In the 1494 Treaty of Tordesillas, the world had been divided into two areas: one for Portugal and one for Spain. Since no one had ever sailed around the world, it was uncertain where the division line lay on the far side of the globe. Magellan believed that some of the Spice Islands might lie on the Spanish side of the line, and he intended to sail there to prove it. The Spanish king knew that if Magellan was right, it could mean great riches for Spain. He agreed to support Magellan's plan.

When Magellan's expedition left Spain in September 1519, trouble was already brewing on his five ships. Spanish captains and sailors were not happy that a Portuguese upstart had been placed in command. There was talk of rebellion and mutiny before the fleet even began its Atlantic crossing. But the five ships managed to cross the Atlantic and reach the coast of Brazil in December. Magellan's troubles would soon grow.

The new year had passed, and it was March 1520 when Magellan's fleet was sailing down the coast of South America. Rebellious feelings among the other captains and sailors came to an explosive head. The captain of one of the ships, the *Concepción*, boarded and seized another of the ships, the *San Antonio*. A full-blown mutiny was under way. Magellan acted quickly, and with enough men still supporting him, he was able to stop the rebellion. Some of the offenders were put to death, and one was marooned. Unwilling to lose sight of his goal, Magellan ordered his fleet to continue sailing south to look for the westerly strait that would lead through South America to the ocean on the other side. Though one of the ships was wrecked off the Patagonian shore, near present-day Argentina, they continued searching for the route west.

In October, they found it. Investigating a wide inlet, the ships navigated a narrow passage that led to another bay in the distance. It

Portrait of Ferdinand Magellan

was indeed the strait Magellan had claimed they would find, a passage now named in his honor. They sailed through it and emerged into the wide ocean on the other side. However, the crew's dissatisfaction had not subsided, and the *San Antonio* turned east and sailed back in the direction of Spain with most of the party's provisions. The three remaining ships idled at the Creek of Sardines, collecting food. Noting how calm this western ocean seemed, Magellan named it the Pacific, or peaceful, Ocean. Contemporary thought held that this Pacific Ocean was small. But as Magellan and his fleet turned northwest to sail across it, they discovered just how vast the Pacific really was.

As one month gave way to the next and the next, the ships made slow progress in the sparse wind. Though the sailors spotted islands in the distance several times, they were unable to make landfall. The temperature had become brutally hot. Meat was rotting in the ships' holds, and the water supply had become tainted and foul. Maggots infested everything. Lacking a crucial supply of fresh fruit and vegetables, the men began to sicken and die from malnutrition. This condition was called scurvy, and in Magellan's time no one knew that it resulted from a lack of vitamin C. All the men knew was that it was a brutal, wasting disease that killed them in great numbers.

In March, the fleet finally reached the island of Guam and obtained food. The mariners and the natives regarded each other with suspicion and dislike. Accusing them of stealing, Magellan ordered several of the natives killed. The ships hastily departed, continuing to the Philippines and stopping at an island called Mactan. Here Magellan paused to educate the natives in Christianity and to look for gold. Magellan seems to have become caught up in a local dispute, and he unwisely agreed to help one side. Leading an attack on a chief named Lapu Lapu, Magellan was struck repeatedly by spears and died. His men were unable to recover his body and had to leave him there.

The remaining survivors organized themselves as best they could. They wanted to return to Spain, but turning back and recrossing the Pacific was out of the question. They would have to continue forward, around the globe, and return home by way of circumnavigation. Of the three ships left, one was badly damaged and had to be burned. After passing the Spice Islands, the ship *Trinidad* was captured by the Portuguese. Only the *Victoria* and her small, starving crew of eighteen survived to return to Spain on September 6, 1522.

Magellan had sought the key to the globe, and his passage through the Strait of Magellan unlocked the world. Though it was never his intention to circumnavigate the globe, he is directly responsible for that monumental achievement. As to his original goal, he had proved that sailing west to the Spice Islands was not a viable choice. The distance was simply too great. In the Age of Discovery, Magellan is yet another example of an explorer who won fame and immortality for something he never intended to do.

The Line of Demarcation

Based on Columbus's discoveries, Spain wanted to establish exclusive rights to explore the western Atlantic. Locked in a fierce competition to discover and claim new lands, Portugal and Spain fought for the chance to dominate the world. Since both nations were Catholic, the question went before Pope Alexander VI. His solution was simple and outrageous in its complete lack of acknowledgment of any nations or people outside his dominion. The Pope simply divided the world in two by establishing an imaginary line of demarcation around the globe. Land west of the line, unless it was a territory already under Christian rule, would belong to Spain. Portugal argued about the placement of the line, and as a result of the Treaty of Tordesillas in 1494, the line moved one thousand miles and Portugal was content to lay claim to everything that lay east of the new line. Since the exact circumference of the earth had never been measured, it was impossible for geographers to plot the location of the line of demarcation around the globe. Where it actually lay on the far side of the earth was a matter of debate. But no matter how murky the details, the Treaty of Tordesillas is a perfect example of the sense of entitlement borne by exploring nations in the Age of Discovery. As they saw it, and as the authority of the Pope confirmed, regardless of any native peoples they found, the world was theirs for the taking.

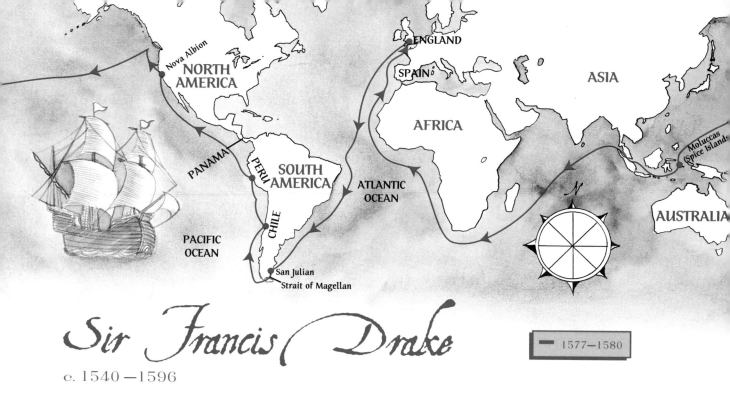

Sir Francis Drake

1577–1580

c. 1540 –1596

When Sir Francis Drake completed his circumnavigation of the world in 1580, he arrived home in England on a ship bursting with treasure and gifts for Queen Elizabeth I. The inspiration for his expedition was the quest for riches and power, but its seeds may have been planted in Drake's childhood hatred of everything Spanish.

Francis Drake was the eldest of twelve sons born to a Protestant farmer when England was ruled by Mary I, later known as Bloody Mary. Mary's father, King Henry VIII, had broken with Roman Catholicism and reorganized an independent English (or Anglican) church. Mary wanted England to return to the Catholic faith and persecuted Protestants relentlessly. Because of the rioting and violent unrest, Drake's family was forced to leave their farm. Drake's father became a Protestant preacher, and Drake himself went to sea as a young teenager. This was a time when England was beginning to grow as a sea power, although the supreme nation was Spain. When England's new queen, Elizabeth I, returned the country to the Protestant faith, England and Catholic Spain became enemies.

In his twenties, Drake worked on trading ships, making several slaving journeys to Africa and the Caribbean. On one such trip he survived a Spanish attack that could only have furthered his hatred of Spain. Following these voyages, Drake began to profit less as a trader and more as a privateer, or raider, of rival Spanish ships. On one of his raiding expeditions in 1572, Drake captured an enormous amount of Spanish silver in Central America. It is little wonder the Spanish called him El Draco, or The Dragon. While in Panama, the narrow land linking the continents of North and South America, Drake had his first glimpse of the Pacific Ocean. When he returned to England, his ship heavy with captured Spanish treasure, Drake's personal share made him a very rich man. He began to formulate a daring new plan.

Queen Elizabeth I was well aware of King Philip II of Spain's growing difficulties. As he focused more and more of his military and financial resources on his quest to reestablish Catholicism in Europe, Philip's money and manpower were running low. So when Drake proposed that he sail a fleet of ships to the New World, pass through the Strait of Magellan, and plunder the Spanish ships and settlements on the Pacific coast of South America, Elizabeth approved. Drake would also search for the Northwest Passage, but it was understood that his most important aim was to rob the Spanish. Elizabeth knew that if Drake could help stop the flow of South American treasure into Spain, it would be a painful blow to King Philip and a welcome source of money for England.

Drake set sail at the end of 1577 with a fleet of five ships. Before even reaching South America, Drake took several prizes: a Portuguese ship carrying valuable supplies and the ship's pilot, who was extremely familiar with sailing conditions and currents in the Atlantic Ocean. The fleet reached the port of San Julian, in present-day Argentina, in June 1578. Here, in view of the trees on which Magellan had hung his mutineers over fifty years earlier, Drake encountered his own rebellion. A nobleman accompanying the expedition, Thomas Doughty, had grown unhappy with his lack of authority. He had been spreading feelings of dissatisfaction among the men on his ship, the *Mary*. Drake charged the young courtier with mutiny. A hastily created court found him guilty. After dining with Drake and wishing the expedition good fortune, Doughty was executed.

By September, they had passed through the Strait of Magellan. The three remaining ships were now in the Pacific Ocean. Of the original five, one had sunk in the stormy waters of the strait and a second had turned back to England without permission. Drake's ship, the *Pelican*, had been given a new name: the *Golden Hind*. It would become one of the most famous ships of the age. Having reached their intended destination on the western

Engraving of Sir Francis Drake

coast of South America, Drake and his vessels began their attacks. On the coasts of Chile and Peru, silver was practically theirs for the asking. Drake robbed ships and harbors methodically as his fleet moved north. Though two Spanish warships were now searching for Drake, El Draco would not take his eye off the magnificent prize that lay ahead.

She was the *Nuestra Señora de la Concepción,* nicknamed by her men the *Cacafuego*. On one of his raids, Drake had heard about this ship, which was carrying tons of silver. During this period of time, Spanish convoy ships regularly transported gold, silver, and other treasures obtained in the Spanish colonies in the Americas back to Spain. It was customary for the collected treasures to be transferred to present-day Colombia or Panama, beginning the return trip to Spain in the spring with Spanish warships as an escort. Instead of launching an all-out attack, Drake hoisted a Spanish flag and disguised his ship as a Spanish merchant vessel. It was not until he was bearing down on the unsuspecting *Nuestra Señora* that Drake began firing his cannons. The battle was over very quickly, and twenty-six tons of silver and a wealth of other prizes were transferred to the *Golden Hind*. By today's standards, the haul was worth tens of millions of dollars.

With no intention of waiting until the Spanish warships found him, Drake sailed north long enough to make a brief look for the legendary gateway to the Atlantic, the Northwest Passage. He traveled up the coast of present-day California, going ashore in June 1579 to make repairs to his ships and claiming the area, which he called Nova Albion, in the name of the queen. The location of Drake's Nova Albion is not known. It may lie in the region north of present-day San Francisco. With no success finding the passage, Drake was in a hurry to be on the move. Although it was probably never his intention to circumnavigate the world, it was too dangerous to go back across the Atlantic. So the fleet continued west, crossing the Pacific Ocean and stopping briefly in the Spice Islands to buy cloves and to reprovision.

Every man in the fleet was now potentially wealthy due to their enormous haul. But their futures were threatened when the *Golden Hind* ran aground on a reef after leaving the Spice Islands. After they tossed many of their supplies and all of the valuable cloves overboard, the *Golden Hind* was light enough to float off the reef and sailed once again for England. When they reached Plymouth Harbor, it was September 1580. Drake had just become the first man to command a complete circumnavigation of the globe (Magellan had not lived to complete his own).

Drake brought enormous treasure to the queen. Though authorities in Spain were furious over Drake's thievery, Queen Elizabeth made no secret of her approval of Drake's actions when she knighted him aboard his ship. The strife between England and Spain was now official.

In the years that followed, Drake continued to threaten the Spanish. He was vice admiral of the British fleet that defeated the powerful Spanish Armada in 1588. On the water until the end, Drake died of dysentery on his ship off the coast of Panama in 1596.

The Spanish Inquisition

Sixteenth-century Spain spent considerable money and manpower trying to control a Protestant rebellion and keep the religion of Roman Catholicism supreme in Europe. Since England's Henry VIII broke with Rome and the Pope in 1532 and established the Anglican Church, Spain had fought determinedly to return England to the Roman Catholic faith. But their battle for Catholicism had begun long before England reorganized its church.

In 1478, the Spanish Inquisition was reestablished by Ferdinand and Isabella, monarchs of the Catholic areas of Aragón and Castile in present-day Spain. Like the medieval Inquisition, it was organized to find and punish those guilty of the crime of heresy, or speaking against the official teachings of the Catholic Church. The primary goal of the Inquisition was to punish Jews and Muslims and wipe out those religions in Spanish territories. Other groups, such as Protestants, later became targets of the Inquisition, along with those accused of witchcraft.

The Inquisition ushered in a reign of terror, during which almost anyone could be accused and in which torture and execution at the stake were common. The Spanish Crown took the property of the condemned, enriching itself in the process. Thousands and thousands were put to death during the Spanish Inquisition until it was officially abolished in 1834.

NORTH AMERICA

ATLANTIC OCEAN

PACIFIC OCEAN

SOUTH AMERICA

1519–1520

MEXICO (NEW SPAIN)

GULF OF MEXICO

Cholula

La Villa Rica de la Veracruz (Veracruz)

Yucatán Península

CUBA

HISPANIOLA

Tenochtitlán (City of Dreams)

AZTEC EMPIRE

PACIFIC OCEAN

SOUTH AMERICA

THE AMERICAS

Hernán Cortés
1485–1547

The group of Spanish adventurers known as the conquistadors shared an obsession with gold—tracking it, finding it, and stealing it. The conquistador Hernán Cortés was no exception. His thirst for gold was so tremendous that he stopped at nothing to acquire it. He even told some Indians that he and his men had to eat gold to avoid becoming sick.

Cortés was born in Medellín, Spain, to a noble family. As a young man, he enrolled at the University of Salamanca but later dropped out. Cortés decided to seek his fortune elsewhere. Around the age of nineteen, he followed many of his countrymen to the island of Hispaniola. Shortly thereafter, Cortés settled in Cuba.

The Spanish governor of Cuba, Diego Velázquez, had heard stories that an area called the Yucatán was brimming with gold. The Yucatán was only 120 miles west of Cuba. There were rumors of a rich and breathtaking Aztec capital city in the land's northern reaches. Velázquez asked Cortés to organize an expedition to find out more about the civilization there. Cortés would have to pay for some of the expedition himself, but he would also share in all the profits and treas-

ure. Cortés agreed to the journey and spared no expense in acquiring ships, supplies, and manpower. When Velázquez heard that Cortés had organized eleven ships, over five hundred men, and a variety of dogs and horses (species relatively unknown in the Yucatán area), he realized Cortés was planning a significantly more expensive expedition than originally intended. The governor sent orders to Cortés relieving him of duty. Cortés ignored them and quickly set sail.

Cortés reached the coast of the Yucatán, much of which is in present-day Mexico, in March 1519. There Cortés met Malinche, the woman who would become his companion, his translator, and perhaps his advisor. In addition to her own Mayan language, Malinche was fluent in the tongue of the Aztecs, the civilization that Cortés wished to

Hernán Cortés

reach. Malinche stayed with Cortés throughout his Mexican expedition, and historians think he highly valued her opinions.

Cortés was always scheming and calculating. At a town he named La Villa Rica de la Veracruz (now just Veracruz), he set up a local government and had himself elected captain-general so that he was now officially under Spanish authority. Since Governor Velázquez had stripped Cortés of his authority, it was a clever move. Velázquez would be hard-pressed to stop Cortés if he was acting in the name of the king. Cortés and his men set off to the north, toward central Mexico.

Montezuma, the emperor of the Aztecs, sent a messenger to Cortés. Montezuma had heard stories about these white-faced men from the east. Whether he believed that they were gods or was concerned about their reputation for violence, Montezuma chose to be welcoming. Cortés accepted the messenger's gifts and responded that he and his men were on their way to see Montezuma.

Encouraged by the lack of threat from the natives, Cortés gave the astonishing order that his ships be destroyed. This prevented his men from rebelling and returning to Cuba, where Cortés was now considered an outlaw. Since he claimed to be acting directly for the Spanish Crown, Cortés set out to use his authority to conquer the Aztec capital two hundred miles away.

His march took him through many native Indian towns ruled by the Aztecs. Since many of these small territories resented Montezuma's rule, Cortés took the opportunity to befriend them. He encouraged their resistance toward the Aztecs while assuring Montezuma's messengers and emissaries that he wished for peace.

In the city of Cholula, Cortés displayed his ruthless and violent nature. Malinche had heard a rumor that the Cholulans planned to capture Cortés and kill all his men. Without seeking any evidence, Cortés and his followers killed several thousand unarmed Cholulans who were meeting at a temple.

By November, the Spanish had reached the Aztec capital city of Tenochtitlán, the City of Dreams. This city of bridges, temples, and towers was indeed beautiful beyond Cortés's dreams. Here Cortés came face to face with Montezuma for the first time, taking him prisoner soon after.

In April 1520, Cortés's past was catching up with him. Word reached the conquistador that a representative of Governor Velázquez had landed on the Yucatán Peninsula with orders to find and capture Cortés. Leaving one of his men in charge of Tenochtitlán, Cortés marched with a large number of his men to head off Velázquez's loyal conquistadors. After a short battle, Cortés emerged the victor. He had, however, stayed away from the City of Dreams for too long.

During Cortés's absence, his men's violent behavior had stirred up enormous resentment among the locals. The Aztecs were feeling rebellious, but whether they had any definite plans to attack the Spanish is not clear. Apparently fearful of an attack, the Spanish temporary leader, Alvarado, instructed his men to march to a temple where a crowd was celebrating the Aztec spring festival. The Aztecs had no chance to fight back in the bloodbath that followed.

By the time Cortés returned, the City of Dreams was in a complete uproar. Cortés ordered Montezuma to appear before his people and plead for them to be peaceful. The Spanish account says that during this appearance, the angry Aztecs threw stones at Montezuma, killing him. However, some historians believe Cortés had Montezuma put to death. The mob was so angry and out of control that Cortés was forced to flee the city with the remainder of his people. He returned in August 1521 to reconquer the City of Dreams. This second invasion, coupled with a vicious outbreak of the smallpox virus, devastated the Aztec civilization.

Cortés was honored for his bloody achievements and made governor of Mexico, then called New Spain. He spent his last years sponsoring expeditions and searching for a sea passage through the continent to link the Atlantic and Pacific oceans. He returned to Spain in 1540. When he died in 1547, he was secure in his reputation as one of Spain's most ambitious and accomplished conquistadors, and he is remembered in Mexico with anger as one who single-handedly affected the course of history in Central America.

The Aztecs

The Aztecs are often only remembered as a bloodthirsty people who relied on human sacrifice to appease their gods, but they were also very sophisticated and accomplished. The Aztec civilization began as a tribe of Indians who settled in central Mexico in the twelfth century. They did not rise as a power until the fifteenth century, when their capital city of Tenochtitlán became the center of the Aztec empire. When Cortés and the Spanish first came to Tenochtitlán, they were mesmerized by the Aztecs' art and jewelry and amazed at the architecture and engineering of the capital city, built on and around a small island and connected to the mainland by bridges and causeways.

The Aztecs were frequently at war with their neighbors, incorporating conquered tribes into the Aztec empire. They gained large numbers of prisoners of war, who made up the major source of victims for religious ceremonies and sacrifices. The Aztecs worshiped many gods, the most important of which was the god of war, Huitzilopochtli.

Within several years of the arrival of the Spanish, the Aztec empire was no more. The conquistador Cortés brought many weapons and men with him. The Spanish also brought sheep that ate the natives' food. But the most deadly weapon was unintentional. The Aztecs had no knowledge of or resistance to smallpox, and they fell in huge numbers to this disease. With these disadvantages, the fate of the Aztec empire was sealed.

This Aztec mask of the god Xochipilli now sits in the National Museum of Anthropology, Mexico.

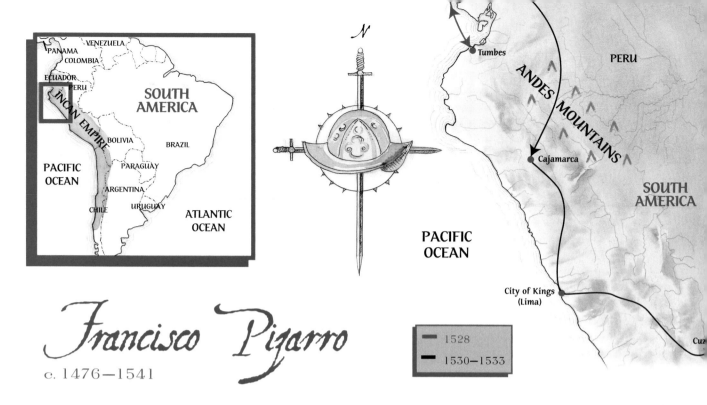

Francisco Pizarro

c. 1476–1541

Like his countryman Hernán Cortés, Francisco Pizarro emerged from being unknown in Spain to standing at the threshold of a great South American kingdom—his to conquer, plunder, and rule.

Born in Spain around the year 1476, Pizarro lived with his soldier father and his mother, a farmer's daughter. Though most of his early life has escaped the history books, we do know that he was poor, he did not go to school, and he could neither read nor write. In the age of the Spanish conquistador, these were obstacles that could be overcome in the New World. Like so many of his countrymen, Pizarro left Spain for the West Indies, settling on the island of Hispaniola. In 1509, he joined an exploratory expedition to the Gulf of Urabá, on the northwest coast of Colombia. From there, Pizarro settled in Panama, the small strip of land connecting South America to Central America.

Pizarro was soon one of the richest and most powerful men in Panama, and his reputation as an explorer was already established. The governor of Panama, Pedro Arias de Avila, asked him to take an expedition down the coast of South America in search of a legendary kingdom of riches.

The first several times Pizarro pushed south with his two ships, he ran into more trouble than success. The conditions were brutal. Mangrove swamps blocked exploration on foot, and clouds of mosquitoes tortured his men as they sailed. The 160-person group encountered a small trading craft carrying Inca goods, mostly silver, gold, and precious jewels. In spite of the bad conditions, the sight was enough to convince Pizarro to continue. He ordered his men to camp on a deserted island off the Colombian coast. One of Pizarro's two ships was sent back to Panama for supplies along with eighty of the men. The ship also carried a secret note to the governor of Panama from some rebellious men, asking to be rescued from Pizarro's group.

By August 1527, a boat from Panama arrived as requested. In a now legendary gesture, Pizarro drew a line in the sand with his sword, telling those who wished to be rich and powerful to cross the line and stand with him. Of the approximately eighty men remaining, only thirteen chose to accompany Pizarro. The rest sailed back to Panama. Pizarro, a man of massive will and determination, remained firm in his ambitions. He resolved to wait for a new ship to be sent to them from Panama. They waited seven months until the ship arrived. It was a long and miserable time for the men, who were sick, starving, and attacked by insects.

Pizarro sailed for only twenty days before the Inca town of Tumbes came into view on the coast of Peru. A party of Spaniards was sent ashore, to the Incas' amazement and curiosity. A highly isolated civilization, the Incas had never encountered Europeans. The Incas gave food and gifts to the Spaniards. Pizarro had brought along an interpreter, and the excited Incas asked question after question about where the Spanish lived and what they were doing so far from home. Welcoming crowds gathered to see the strange men. Some of Pizarro's men were so deeply affected by the beauty of the people and their architecture that they wanted to stay and live with the Incas. Pizarro, anxious to return to Panama to raise an army, allowed two to stay behind.

In spite of his peaceful exchange with the Incas of Tumbes, it is probable that Pizarro's only intention was to return as quickly as possible with an armed group to conquer them. He realized that he had found a highly developed and rich civilization. With the support of Spanish royalty, Pizarro organized an army of 180 men. By December 1530, Pizarro again set sail from Panama in the direction of Peru, landing north of his goal in Ecuador.

It was an unsettled time for the Incas. Smallpox had reached Peru. The Inca leader, Wayna Capac, had died of the disease before choosing his successor. Two of his sons, Atahuallpa and Huascar, began a civil war to determine who would be the new ruler. By the time Pizarro and his small army began

Engraving of Francisco Pizarro

marching toward the Andes mountains, the Inca civilization was already severely weakened by civil war and smallpox.

After crossing the mountains, Pizarro headed for Cajamarca, where the victorious Atahuallpa was rumored to be staying. In November 1532, the Spanish conquistadors and the Incas came face to face. Again communicating through an interpreter, Pizarro made no mention of his intention to attack and conquer the Incas. Atahuallpa probably also intended to capture Pizarro and his men, never dreaming that the 180 Spaniards would be any match for thousands and thousands of Incas. Pizarro demanded that the Incas give up their gods for Christianity. When Atahuallpa rejected the offer and threw the proffered Bible to the ground, Pizarro gave the order to attack.

Unprepared and helpless against the Spanish guns and crossbows, several thousand of the Incas were quickly killed. The remainder, including Atahuallpa, were taken prisoner. Pizarro met no significant resistance during the rest of his attack. Atahuallpa produced a room filled with gold as ransom for his own release, but he was executed anyway. By November 1533, Pizarro had taken the Inca capital, Cuzco. He had also plundered unbelievable treasure, melting down gold walls and statues and remaking them into bricks. Triumphant, Pizarro founded a new capital named the City of Kings. Today it is known as Lima. The people killed and the treasures plundered, Inca civilization was at an end.

Supporters of a rival conquistador killed Pizarro in 1541. The Spanish would thrive in Peru without him, and one period in Peruvian history closed as another began.

The Inca Empire

People have inhabited the dramatic highlands around the Andes mountains for many thousands of years. By the thirteenth century, the various indigenous tribes in and surrounding Peru had united under a single ruler known as the Inca. The Inca empire stretched along the coast of South America, through Peru, north to present-day Ecuador, and south to present-day Chile and Argentina, along with parts of Bolivia.

The Incas relied on farming and herding for most of their food and clothing, developing special techniques to survive on the steep mountainsides. The Incas herded llamas and alpacas and grew fruits, corn, beans, chilies, and potatoes. In addition, the Incas were superb architects and engineers. Their capital city of stone, Cuzco, was linked to the farthest reaches of the empire by stone roads and suspension bridges. The most important buildings in each town and city were the temples.

Religion was the center of Inca life. Elaborate ceremonies took place at temples and street altars. The Incas prayed to their primary god, Viracocha, for everything from health and plentiful harvests to victory over enemies. The Incas also practiced human sacrifice, though less frequently than the Aztecs. An offering of food was much more common.

The Inca empire was at its peak when Pizarro and the Spanish conquest destroyed it. Much of the magnificent architecture and countless musical and artistic creations were lost forever when this mountain civilization and last great American Indian empire was brought to an end.

Present-day Cuzco, former capital of the Inca empire

NOUVELLE FRANCE
(QUÉBEC)

Strait of Belle Isle

Stadacona
(Québéc City)
Cap-Rouge
Orléans

NEW
BRUNSWICK

Bay of Gaspé

Prince Edward
Island

NEWFOUNDLAND

St. Lawrence
River

Hochelaga
Mont-Réal
(Montreal)

ATLANTIC
OCEAN

CANADA

NORTH
AMERICA

ATLANTIC
OCEAN

PACIFIC
OCEAN

1534
1535—1536

Jacques Cartier

1491–1557

When King Francis I of France met Jacques Cartier, he was impressed by Cartier's reputation as a capable seaman. He had grown up in the famous Brittany seaport of Saint-Malo, where great ships and the sea were a way of life. Cartier was already a seasoned transatlantic sailor, and the king asked him to head a French voyage of discovery to the New World.

Like the other European countries, France saw the enormous value of a northwest passage linking the Atlantic and Pacific oceans. Cartier believed one might exist in the northern reaches of the North American continent, beyond what fishermen called the Strait of Belle Isle, off the coast of Newfoundland.

Cartier outfitted two ships and embarked from France in April 1534. He made the Atlantic crossing in just twenty days, reaching Newfoundland on May 10. By June, he had sailed through the Strait of Belle Isle into uncharted waters, moving down the west coast of Newfoundland to beautiful Prince Edward Island. Sailing north up the New Brunswick coast, Cartier had one of his first encounters with Indians. The Micmac were enthusiastic about exchanging goods.

More significant was Cartier's meeting with the Huron people in the Bay of Gaspé. Chief Donnaconna and his people had traveled east from their home to fish. When Cartier erected a giant cross and a sign reading "Long Live the French King" on the land, Donnaconna protested. But Cartier gave him gifts and lessened his anxiety. Donnaconna even agreed to send his two sons, Domagaya and Taignoaguy, with Cartier on a visit across the sea to France. By September 1534, the expedition had returned home, to the king's great excitement. Spain had already made huge claims in the New World, and France wanted some land of its own.

Within months, Cartier had authorization to begin preparing a new expedition. He obtained three ships and organized 112 men. By September 1, 1535, the expedition was sailing into the mouth of the St. Lawrence

A depiction of Cartier's first encounter with the Indians at Hochelaga in 1535

City. Donnaconna tried to talk Cartier out of sailing farther west with both stories of devils and bad omens to the west and tales of a rich kingdom called Saguenay in the interior. In reality, Donnaconna wanted to be France's main ally and did not want Cartier making friends with his rival Hurons upriver.

But Cartier ignored Donnaconna's pleas and sailed west with a small party, leaving the rest of his men and boats behind. On October 2, 1535, Cartier reached Hochelaga, where he was enthusiastically welcomed by over a thousand Hurons. Cartier explored the island and climbed a local mountain. He named it Mont-Réal, for which today's city of Montreal is named. From the summit, Cartier could see

River. Cartier named the islands they saw as they sailed upriver. At a large island he named Orléans, Domagaya and Taignoaguy were reunited with their father, Chief Donnaconna. The chief's people lived on the northern bank of the river in a place called Stadacona, the location of today's Québec

Modern-day Québec City

that the St. Lawrence River continued to the west. But he could also see a series of violent rapids that would make passage by his ships impossible.

Cartier and his party returned to Stadacona and spent the winter there. It was a long and brutally cold season, and twenty-five of Cartier's men died of scurvy. They all might have died had Domagaya not paid them a visit. He showed them a tree that contained high amounts of vitamin C. Domagaya prepared a potion from the tree's bark, and the rest of the men recovered.

When it was time to return to France, Cartier had begun to suspect that Donnaconna was planning to attack. With this justification in mind, he kidnapped Donnaconna and four other Hurons. Cartier took the five captives and five other Indians on the return trip to France, but none survived to return home.

The king sent Cartier on one final expedition in 1541 to establish a French colony in Canada. He placed a nobleman, Jean-François de Roberval, in charge. But Roberval was not ready to depart and ordered Cartier and his ships to proceed alone. Attempting to create a colony at Cap-Rouge, Cartier found the local Indians increasingly unfriendly. By June 1542, Indian raids forced Cartier to give up and sail for home. He was surprised to find Roberval's ships at Newfoundland, having just arrived after departing a year late from France. Against Roberval's orders, Cartier returned with his ships to France but did not suffer for his disobedience.

Cartier spent his last years quietly in Saint-Malo, a celebrated local hero and discoverer of the St. Lawrence River. He had opened the door of the New World for the people of France.

The Scourge of Scurvy

Of all the dangers sixteenth-century explorers faced, one of the most deadly was scurvy. It was a wasting and often lethal sickness of then unknown cause. Beginning with aches and pains in the joints and teeth that became loose in blackening gums, scurvy progressed rapidly. Victims were covered in purple blotches, with the disease weakening the blood vessels and sapping the strength from swelling limbs. Often becoming mentally demented, the victim would experience increasing pain and decreasing strength, finally losing the ability to eat. Death soon followed.

Scurvy was a common visitor on almost any lengthy sea voyage. The crews of explorers Ferdinand Magellan and Vasco da Gama were devastated by it. Yet in spite of the 100 percent effective cure made by the Hurons and given to Cartier's men, the cause of and remedy for scurvy were not fully understood until the eighteenth century. It was revealed that the disease was not a contagious illness like smallpox but rather was the result of a poor diet. Scurvy was caused by the absence of vitamin C, found in citrus fruits such as oranges and limes as well as tomatoes, green peppers, and other fresh fruits and vegetables.

Ships' rations relied heavily on ground meal and salted meats, neither of which provided vitamin C. When the British navy began issuing limes as part of their ships' rations, the disease disappeared almost completely.

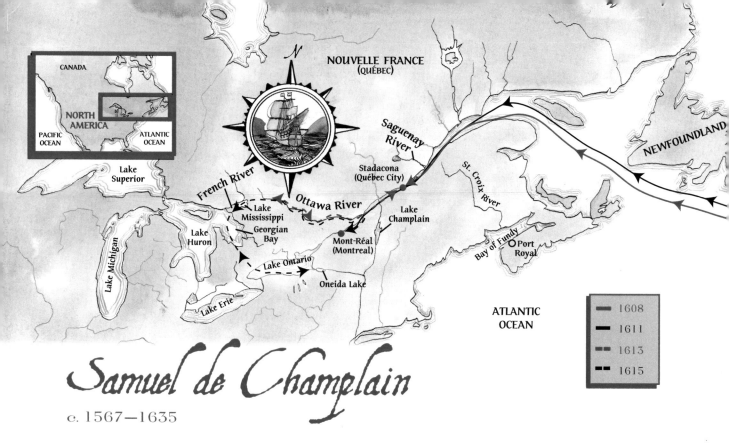

Samuel de Champlain
c. 1567–1635

When Samuel de Champlain was a young adult, French fishermen had been working and trading off the coast of Newfoundland for years. But there had not been any French land gains on the continent since Cartier's failed colony in the 1540s. The large amount of fur available for trade to French fishermen got the attention of King Henry IV. Clearly there was profit to be made in the New World. The French king decided that it was time for France to establish a firmer presence in the territory.

A sea captain's son, Samuel de Champlain was raised in the seaport town of Brouage. He served for a time in the army and later gained navigational experience traveling to Spain with his uncle and to the West Indies on a trade ship. When Aymar de Chaste organized a colonizing expedition to Canada in 1603, he invited Champlain to join.

During that trip to Canada, Champlain undertook several journeys up the St. Lawrence and Saguenay rivers, noting that Cartier's old site of Stadacona would make a good place for a colony. However, the first colony was begun on an island in the St. Croix River, then moved to a second site across the Bay of Fundy at Port Royal.

Due to harsh weather and poor diet, the colonies were not successful.

In 1608, Champlain made a second journey to the New World, this time commanding three ships. He returned to Stadacona, which he called Québec, and chose a site to begin building a fort for a new colony. This was the first permanent French settlement in Canada.

During the following years, Champlain divided his time between mapping the Canadian interior and making trips back to France. Here he renewed support and funding for his colony, now known as Nouvelle France. The king was pleased with Champlain's discoveries, including an enormous lake over one hundred miles long now named Lake Champlain.

By 1611, France had a new king, Louis XIII. Champlain had to return to France to make sure he had the new king's support. While there, Champlain was able to secure a new commission that gave him complete authority over the affairs of the Nouvelle France colony. With his position secure, Champlain returned to Canada. He built a preliminary wall at Mont-Réal with the intention of establishing a trading post there. By now, Champlain had made a successful alliance with the Huron and Algonquin Indians. In order to keep this relationship healthy, he proclaimed their enemies, the Iroquois, to be his enemies as well.

In 1613, Champlain had a great triumph when he paddled up the Ottawa River, successfully navigating a series of very difficult rapids that had been thought impassable. In 1615, Champlain had made his way up the Mattawa and French rivers to Huron territory, on Lake Huron's eastern shore.

Hostilities with the Iroquois were increasing, and Champlain now began recruiting Indian volunteers for an army intended to raid and attack the Iroquois. The battle took place south of Oneida Lake, and Champlain and his army were defeated. Following this failure, Champlain returned to Nouvelle France and spent his remaining years running and safeguarding his colony. This included a period of years, between 1628 and 1632, when Nouvelle France was captured and occupied by the British.

Though deeply stung by his failure to win his war against the Iroquois, Champlain had done more to inform France of the landscape and makeup of Canada and the Great Lakes than anyone else. Champlain's legacy of the French language and culture is still evident in Canada today.

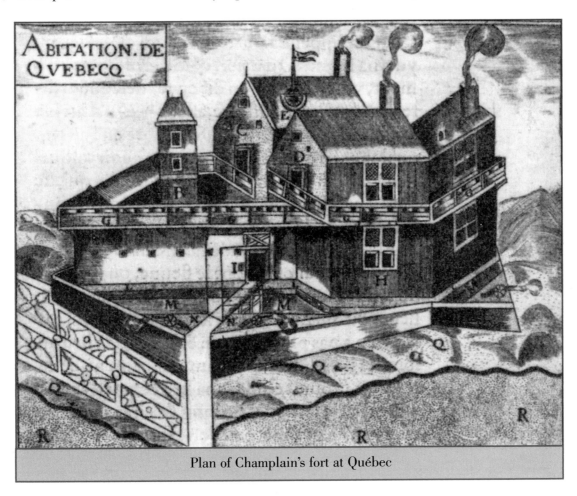

Plan of Champlain's fort at Québec

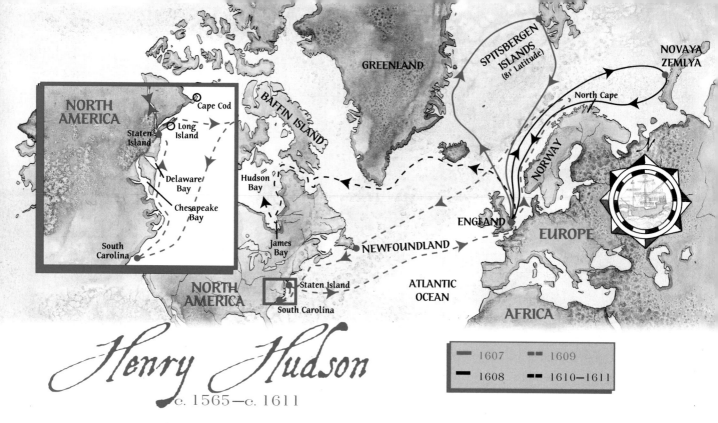

GREENLAND

SPITSBERGEN ISLANDS (81° Latitude)

NOVAYA ZEMLYA

BAFFIN ISLAND

North Cape

NORWAY

NORTH AMERICA

Cape Cod

Long Island

Staten Island

Delaware Bay

Chesapeake Bay

Hudson Bay

South Carolina

James Bay

ENGLAND

EUROPE

NEWFOUNDLAND

NORTH AMERICA

Staten Island

South Carolina

ATLANTIC OCEAN

AFRICA

Henry Hudson
c. 1565—c. 1611

— 1607	-- 1609		
━ 1608	▬▬ 1610—1611		

Like so many of the greatest early explorers, the details surrounding the birth and death of Henry Hudson are unclear. Perhaps the greatest mystery associated with Hudson is his disappearance. Set adrift with his son and several others in a small boat south of the vast Hudson Bay, the explorer was never seen again.

Henry Hudson's story began in England, where he was born around the year 1565. We know little about his life before he undertook his first major expedition in 1607. Although many nations had been searching since the time of Columbus, the race to find a sea passage to the riches of Asia still consumed Portugal, Spain, England, France, Holland, and others. The Muscovy Company was an organization of English merchants who combined resources to fund exploratory journeys that might open profitable new trade routes. They thought that ships might be able to get to trade posts in Asia faster by sailing north of Scandinavia and Russia, instead of west through the Pacific Ocean or south around the tip of Africa. The Muscovy Company hired Hudson to find this northeast passage to Asia.

Hudson's first expedition left England on the *Hopewell* in May 1607. They sailed all the way to the northern archipelago of Spitsbergen before the ice forced them to turn back. Though he had not made any significant headway in finding a northeast passage, Hudson had reached a latitude of 81 degrees, farther north than any European was known to have voyaged before him.

The Muscovy Company also funded Hudson's second expedition. With a crew of fifteen manning one ship, Hudson again set off in search of the Northeast Passage. This time he headed north up the Norwegian coast and bypassed Spitsbergen by sailing east of it. But ice and bitter cold were grave obstacles. The party reached two large islands in the Arctic Ocean called Novaya Zemlya, where once again the ice proved too thick for continued progress to the northeast. Before turning back, Hudson wrote a statement saying that he was going home of his own free will, not because of any pressure from the crew. The fact that he wrote such a statement indicates there was certainly some rebellion by the crew.

Since his first two expeditions had not significantly advanced the search for the Northeast Passage, the Muscovy Company lost interest in Hudson. But the Dutch East India Company quickly hired him. They wanted Hudson to continue where he had left off in Novaya Zemlya, finding a way to continue around to the northeast. They provided Hudson with a contract specifically stating these goals and requiring that he not make any departure from the plan.

In March 1609, Hudson set sail on the *Half Moon*. He again sailed up the Norwegian coast, but at North Cape, a combination of ice and violent storms brought the ship to a halt. Hudson did not retrace his route back to England but instead turned the ship west and sailed across the Atlantic to the New World. There are different theories as to why. One suggestion is that the crew had mutinied and forced Hudson to go west. Another theory is that Hudson had been paid by the English to ruin the Dutch attempt at the Northeast Passage. It is also possible that Hudson took it upon himself to head west, in search of a northwest passage.

By July 1609, the *Half Moon* had reached Newfoundland. The expedition sailed down the North American coast as far as present-day South Carolina before Hudson turned the ship around and began to sail back north. In September, the expedition reached present-day Staten Island and explored New York Harbor. Here Hudson met at length with local Indians who lived along a large river that extended to the north. Hudson decided to explore the river, which now bears his name. He was able to take his ship over one hundred miles upriver and was near present-day Albany when he finally turned back. This was the first ascent of the Hudson River by any European explorer. Following his return to New York Harbor, Hudson took the *Half Moon* directly back to England.

Hudson's fourth and final voyage was once again on behalf of the English. Backed by another London merchants' association, Hudson was given a ship called *Discovery* and a crew of twenty-two men. Only a small section of Hudson's journal has survived to provide details about the final voyage and its mysterious ending. *Discovery* set out in April 1610 to search for a northwest passage. *Discovery* sailed west past Greenland before passing between Baffin Island to the north and the coast of Canada to the south. The ship came to a massive bay, now named after Hudson. Though there was trouble with both difficult weather conditions and currents, Hudson continued sailing south until he reached James Bay, a small sheltered bay at the south end of present-day Hudson Bay. He announced to his crew that they would spend the winter there, continuing in the spring when the ice had melted enough for them to sail safely. This decision almost caused an instant mutiny, but Hudson maintained control of his men.

The winter at James Bay was long, dark,

Wood engraving of Henry Hudson

and cold, and the crew suffered from a serious lack of supplies. Rumors circulated, accusing Hudson of hiding food for himself. Though spring arrived and the temperatures rose, the rebellious air grew stronger. By June, the ice had melted enough to set sail, but the hostile crew was no longer responding to Hudson's orders. Instead, they tied him up and cast him adrift in a small lifeboat with his son and eight other loyal men. They were given no food and only one musket among them. The little boat and its castaway occupants were never seen or heard from again.

The mutineers did not fare much better, suffering an attack by Indians that killed five of them. A sixth died of starvation before they reached Ireland, leaving only seven survivors out of the original thirteen mutineers. The truth was guarded carefully by the mutineers, and they were never prosecuted. The facts surrounding the final days of Henry Hudson died with the lost castaways.

Sir Walter Raleigh and the Mystery of Roanoke

Henry Hudson was not the only person to be lost without a trace in North America. Sir Walter Raleigh lost an entire colony of people. Raleigh was a brilliant and handsome favorite of Queen Elizabeth I. In 1584, she gave him a royal charter making him land proprietor of a large area in the New World south of Delaware Bay. The stage was set to realize one of Raleigh's most ambitious dreams—the establishment of a New World colony.

The next year, Raleigh organized a group to colonize Roanoke Island, near the border of today's Virginia and North Carolina. Seven ships carrying five hundred colonists set sail from England. When the colonists settled on Roanoke Island, the weather seemed mild and the land capable of supporting a colony. But some settlers set on seeking fortunes made trouble with the local Indians. Short on food, the colonists seized the opportunity to go home when Sir Francis Drake's fleet of ships stopped by to check on them.

Still convinced of Roanoke's great potential, Raleigh simply gathered a new group of colonists. In July 1587, the 117 new colonists arrived in Roanoke. They prospered for a year but then began to run low on supplies. The colony's governor, John White, decided to sail back to England for provisions. Once in England, White's return was delayed due to hostilities with Spain. When White was finally able to go back to Roanoke in 1590, he found that every colonist had vanished without a trace. Among the missing were White's daughter and son-in-law and their baby, Virginia Dare. She was the first English baby born in the New World. The only clue to their fate was the word *Croatan*, the name of a nearby island, carved into a wooden post. A search gave no evidence the colonists ever made it to Croatan.

Though Walter Raleigh's mark was made permanently in Virginia, the disappearance of the original Roanoke colonists remains a mystery.

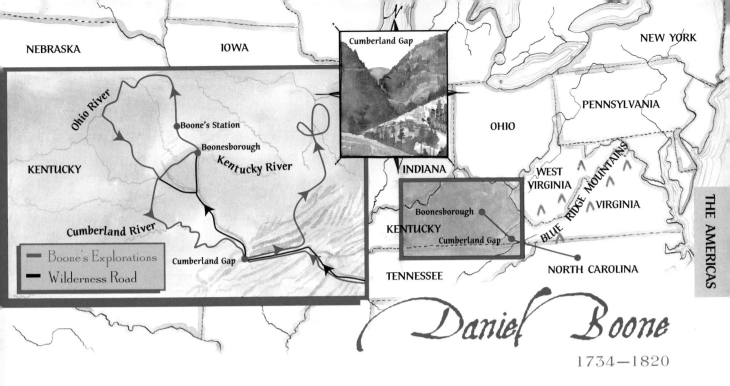

Daniel Boone
1734—1820

The life of Daniel Boone is the stuff of American legend. Though many of the stories of Boone's exploits are fictional, the true events of his life are just as remarkable.

Born in Pennsylvania in 1734, Daniel Boone was one of eleven children in a hearty and close-knit family. He was a gifted hunter, spending much of his childhood exploring the wilderness. His love of solitude and his desire to be far from civilization remained constant throughout his life.

When he was a teenager, Boone's family relocated to North Carolina. Living in the wilds along the Yadkin River, Boone continued to develop his hunting skills. He also fought for the British in the French and Indian War. He began to hear stories of a pristine and captivating wilderness west of the Appalachian Mountains.

He first traveled over the mountains to present-day Kentucky on one of his long hunting expeditions in 1767, but he was not able to make an extended stay until 1769. Organizing a party that included five companions and many horses, Boone journeyed over the Blue Ridge Mountains and north to an old Indian trail, which led through a gateway in the mountains called the Cumberland Gap.

Passing through the gap, Boone and his men left the frontier behind and entered a land untouched by Western settlement. Magnificent wooded vistas overflowing with game captured Boone's heart. He established a permanent camp, not returning to North Carolina until two years later, in 1771.

In North Carolina, Boone and his wife, Rebecca, had a growing family of their own. They encountered the increasing problem of too many settlers and hunters for the available land. Along with seven other families, the Boones set out through the Cumberland Gap to make a new home in Kentucky, but the party was attacked by Indians. Six people were killed, including Boone's eldest son, James. Heartbroken, the family temporarily abandoned their journey.

But Boone's reputation as a formidable scout, hunter, and explorer continued to grow. He became known as a man who did not lose his head in a crisis and who learned from his experiences. Captured by Indians more than once, Boone always emerged unscathed. An avid reader, he carried one of his favorite books, *Gulliver's Travels,* on his Kentucky trips.

Many settlers began to share Boone's interest in Kentucky, and a land agent hired Boone in 1775 to make a road along the old Indian trail through the Cumberland Gap. With a crew of men, Boone cut away fallen trees, cleared underbrush, and built make-shift bridges. The resulting route, called the Wilderness Road, led all the way to the Kentucky River and attracted thousands of families seeking new homes.

Boone organized a settlement and fort called Boonesborough, on the Kentucky River. By the mid-1780s, over thirty thousand people had settled in the territory. After the American Revolution, Boone established a second settlement, now called Boone's Station, north of the Kentucky River. He eventually moved even farther west to Missouri and lived his last years hunting and trapping on the long, quiet trips that he loved.

The Abduction and Rescue of Jemima Boone

*O*ne of the most celebrated and retold Daniel Boone stories centers on his daughter Jemima. In 1776, Boone and his family were living in the settlement of Boonesborough on the Kentucky River. Thirteen-year-old Jemima decided to take a canoe onto the river with two of her friends, fourteen- and sixteen-year-old sisters Fanny and Elizabeth Callaway. Paddling farther away from the settlement than they should have, the three girls were surprised by a group of five Cherokee and Shawnee Indians. Indian resistance to frontier settlers had been growing rapidly, and the Cherokee and Shawnee were among the tribes angered by their displacement. Recognizing that one of the girls was the child of the famous pioneer Daniel Boone, the Indians jumped at the chance for revenge. They sped off with the girls, but not before their shrieks alerted their families back at the settlement.

Hastily gathering a group of men to join him, Boone took off in pursuit of the Indians. The girls had done their best to leave a trail, snapping branches as they were dragged along. Nonetheless, Boone was ten miles behind the children. For three days, Boone and his men fought their way through the brush, desperate to draw closer before the five Indians rejoined their war parties.

In an episode now dramatically re-created in paintings and stories, Boone and his party reached the Indians' encampment at sunset of the third day and crept up on it like panthers. In a flash of gun-powder, they overpowered and scattered the Indians, and the three weeping girls were rescued. Terrified and exhausted, the girls explained that, though they had been pushed at a frightening pace, the Indians had otherwise treated them with kindness. The grateful and relieved men escorted the girls back home. The girls all married within a year of their capture. All three grooms were members of the rescue party that had brought them to safety.

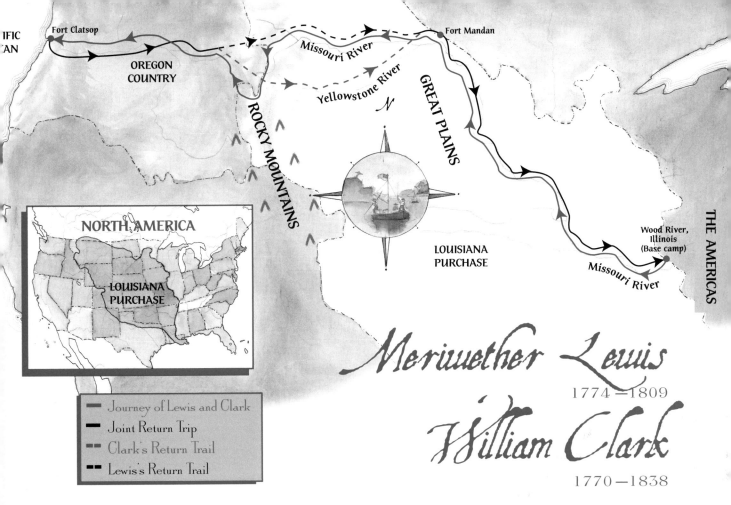

In 1803, the North American continent was covered in pristine wilderness, virtually unexplored by Europeans. At this time, the United States of America extended from the eastern seaboard only to the Mississippi River. But an extraordinary land sale was about to double the country's size. In an exchange called the Louisiana Purchase, France's emperor Napoleon sold more than eight hundred thousand square miles of land to the Americans. However, no one knew what lay within this land. President Jefferson was quick to organize an expedition. He wanted someone to navigate the Missouri River to its source and continue west all the way to the Pacific Ocean. He hoped the fabled Northwest Passage would be found in the process.

President Jefferson chose Captain Meriwether Lewis to lead the expedition, and Lewis picked his army friend Lieutenant William Clark as co-commander. They both were experienced leaders and knew how to survive in the wilderness. Lewis was President Jefferson's personal secretary. He was born and raised in Virginia and had a reputation for being highly capable, serious-minded, and intelligent. William Clark, also born in Virginia, had considerable experience working with Indians in Kentucky and Ohio. Together, especially given their genuine affection for each other, they made a perfect team. They interviewed scores of hopeful explorers, hiring only the best and most experienced to join their Corps of Discovery.

After spending the coldest months of the

winter in their quarters at Wood River in Illinois (near St. Louis, Missouri), the corps departed on May 14, 1804. There were thirty-eight men and three boats—a fifty-five-foot-long keelboat and two small dugout canoes. The boats were packed tightly with supplies, including food, tools, weapons, goods to trade with Indians, and papers and writing instruments for journals and drawings.

Navigating the boats upriver was difficult, with hot, muggy weather and swarms of insects slowing their progress. One man developed appendicitis and died. He would be the only casualty of the entire expedition.

Traveling up the Missouri River past the Great Plains, the corps began encountering Indians, with whom Jefferson wanted to establish good relations. Things began in a friendly way with the Teton Sioux but ultimately became hostile. They were the only

Portrait of Meriwether Lewis by Charles Peale. Mr. Peale also ran a museum in Philadelphia that displayed many of the items collected by the corps on its expedition.

tribe Lewis and Clark failed to befriend on their journey.

Lewis had the corps build their winter quarters among the Mandan Sioux, in present-day North Dakota near the banks of the Missouri River. The Indians helped the corps pass the bitter winter there, and they met a valuable guide for the unknown land ahead—a young Shoshone mother named Sacagawea.

As the corps passed through today's Montana, they sought a Shoshone tribe who could trade them the horses they would need to continue over the Rocky Mountains. With Sacagawea's help, Lewis and Clark found and obtained suitable horses.

The mountains were steep, wet, and cold. Even with the horses, the men barely completed the two-week crossing. They were

Portrait of William Clark by Charles Peale

exhausted and starving when they met Nez Percé Indians on the other side. With the Indians' assistance, the men were able to rest, eat, and recover.

The Missouri River ended east of the Rockies. Now Lewis had new boats built, and the men navigated a series of rivers, the Clearwater, Snake, and Columbia, toward the Pacific Ocean. Despite violent and churning rapids and waterfalls, they made it through. In November 1805, a year and a half after beginning the expedition, the corps saw the Pacific Ocean ahead. They had become the first people known to have crossed the North American continent. Though they had not found the Northwest Passage, they had made valuable contributions to the mapping of the continent's interior, befriended many Indian tribes, and discovered scores of new plant and animal species.

On the long journey back east, Lewis and Clark had to split up for part of the time. But they returned to St. Louis together as heroes. Lewis became the governor of the Louisiana Territory. Unfortunately, his life grew troubled, and he killed himself in 1809. Clark married his longtime sweetheart and became a successful businessman.

Sacagawea

Sacagawea has been immortalized in songs, paintings, books, and movies. The stories of her deeds on the Lewis and Clark expedition have been exaggerated into mere shadows of truth. But Sacagawea was a real person. She was the only woman to join the Corps of Discovery and was an irreplaceable member of the expedition.

As a child, Sacagawea was kidnapped by the neighboring Hidatsa tribe and taken away from her Shoshone home. Eventually she came to live with the Mandan and married a local French Canadian fur trader, Toussaint Charbonneau. When the Corps of Discovery settled in for the winter with the Mandan, Sacagawea was expecting her first child. The labor was difficult, and Lewis made the struggling woman a potion of crushed rattlesnake rings. Shortly after taking it, Sacagawea gave birth to a healthy baby boy.

Some of the more famous paintings and stories of Sacagawea portray her as saving the lost men by directing them to safety. This is largely untrue, but there was much the Shoshone woman actually did do to assist the mission. She was a reliable translator and guide. She was brave and quick-thinking, rescuing the priceless expedition journals when a boat capsized. She helped lead the men to edible plants to add to their diet. And when the corps finally found the Shoshone, Sacagawea's presence enabled the Indians to trust the white men. Incredibly, the Shoshone chief the corps had found was Sacagawea's long-lost brother. They had not seen each other since childhood. Now reunited, the chief was willing to discuss trading horses to the group of men his sister accompanied. Without the horses, the corps could never have continued over the mountains.

Though we know Sacagawea's baby, Jean Baptiste, was eventually adopted and raised by William Clark, Sacagawea herself faded into history, possibly dying with the Mandan in 1812.

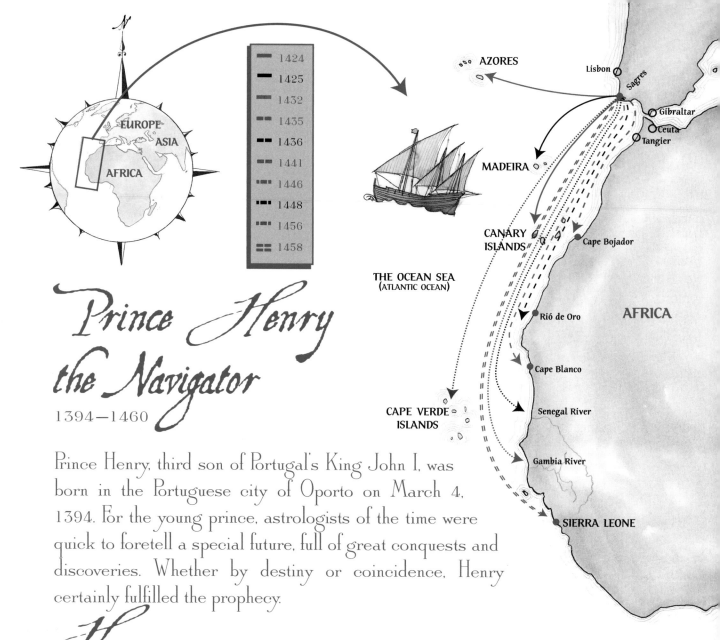

▬▬	1424
▬▬	1425
▬ ▬	1432
▬ ▬	1435
▬▬ ▬▬	1436
▬ ▬	1441
▬▪ ▪▬	1446
▬ ▪▬	1448
▪▪▪ ▪▪	1456
▬▬ ▬▬	1458

Prince Henry the Navigator

1394—1460

Prince Henry, third son of Portugal's King John I, was born in the Portuguese city of Oporto on March 4, 1394. For the young prince, astrologists of the time were quick to foretell a special future, full of great conquests and discoveries. Whether by destiny or coincidence, Henry certainly fulfilled the prophecy.

Henry was raised at court with his brothers in a manner befitting a prince. He was a highly educated boy who showed a devotion to the expansion of the Christian faith. He began his career as a Crusader when he was only twenty-one, helping his father plan and execute an attack on the Muslim city of Ceuta in northern Morocco. After the conquest, the king put Henry in charge of running Ceuta, Portugal's first territorial possession on the African continent. Henry hoped to acquire even more land in Africa.

Henry took up a serious study of maps and charts of the ocean west of Morocco, where the Canary Islands lay. Henry wanted those islands for Portugal, though he knew that Castile already had settlers there. Henry organized a military expedition to the island of Grand Canary in 1424, justifying his actions by saying it was a crusade to convert local islanders to Christianity. However, the locals drove his soldiers off, and Henry's grab for the Canary Islands failed.

Henry was also interested in the islands of Madeira, three hundred miles north of the Canary Island chain. King John began settling Madeira in 1425, probably at Henry's urging. But the king turned his attention in the direction of the mainland when he and Henry had a dispute over whether the Portuguese should attack the Islamic fortress at Gibraltar.

With the power Henry wielded as the king's son, he encouraged mapmaking and shipbuilding. He was actively planning a policy of exploration by way of the Atlantic, referred to on Henry's charts as "the Ocean Sea." Henry wanted to form new trade relationships and also to collect information about African geography and people. He intended to find the "Green Country" of Guinea and perhaps even to locate the legendary kingdom of Prester John (see page 67). As always, Henry stressed the religious nature of his expeditions—every action was in the name of converting the infidels to Christianity.

From his headquarters in Sagres, on the southwest point of Portugal, Prince Henry set his plans into action. Rejecting the commonly held belief that it was dangerous to sail farther south than Cape Bojador, Prince Henry summoned mapmakers, seamen, and scholars to exchange information and develop valid geographical theories about Africa's western coast. He researched mapmaking methods and navigational systems and educated himself in the literature of past travelers. By 1432, his captains had discovered the Azores, a group of islands off Portugal's coast. In 1433, King John died and was succeeded by Henry's older brother, Duarte.

Two years later, Prince Henry sent a ship south for the fifteenth attempt to round Cape Bojador and prove that the world did not end

The Crusades

The Crusades were a series of holy wars launched by Christians against Muslims. Crusaders sought to eliminate the unfaithful, the "infidel," meaning Muslims, Jews, or anyone not practicing Christianity. Crusaders commonly attacked Muslim-held territories in the Holy Land (including modern-day Israel, Jordan, and parts of Egypt) and slaughtered the people living there.

The primary goal of the Crusaders was to capture Muslim-held lands considered sacred to the Christian tradition, such as Jerusalem. The irony is that many of the same sites sacred to the Christian tradition are considered sacred to the Jewish and Muslim faiths as well. Pope Urban II initiated the first Crusade in 1095. Its goal was to free the Holy Sepulchre, the church in Jerusalem that houses Jesus's legendary tomb. The First Crusade ushered in five hundred years of religious warfare. It blazed through Iraq and Syria and into Jerusalem. For Arabs there, it was a shocking and unprovoked assault.

The last of the historical four Crusades in the Holy Land ended in the thirteenth century, but the idea of waging war in the name of Christianity lingered for several hundred years. The struggle of opposing faiths has never been purged from Western or Eastern societies.

Illuminated manuscript depicting the capture of Jerusalem during the First Crusade

beyond it. This time, his men, captained by Gil Eannes, were successful. In proving the legends false, Eannes and his men literally opened a sea and a continent to the Portuguese.

For the next two years, Prince Henry's men were sent to sea with orders to reach as far south as possible. By 1436, Afonso Baldaya passed the mouth of the Rió de Oro, near present-day Western Sahara. But the following year, Henry's energies were diverted to commanding the invasion of the Muslim city of Tangier. The invasion was a disaster. Not only were the Portuguese defeated, but they were forced to promise to return the city of Ceuta to the Muslims. Henry handed over his brother Fernando as collateral. However, Henry never relinquished control of Ceuta, and Fernando died in prison.

King Duarte died in 1438, resulting in a struggle for control of his heir, six-year-old Alfonse V. The resulting chaos prevented Henry from resuming his expeditions until 1441, when Nuno Tristao reached Cape Blanco. That same year, Henry's captain Antao Goncalves reached the area of Rió de Oro and returned to Portugal with African slaves. Henry had long endured criticism that his voyages had no financial payoff, but the slave trade promised to change that. By 1444, one of Henry's men had organized a slave raid. Henry approved the sale of the 240 African men, women, and children, seemingly unmoved by their devastating fate. He reasoned that he was ultimately saving them by bringing them to a Christian culture.

In 1446, Nuno Tristao sailed past the mouth of the Gambia River, in the present-day Republic of the Gambia. Somewhere south of the river, Tristao and his men were killed by a group of African warriors. Prince Henry had lost a valuable man, but there were others to take his place. One of the most important was Venetian-born Alvise da Ca da Mosto, called Cadamosto by the Portuguese. He extensively mapped the coastline around the mouth of the Senegal River, first reached by Henry's men in 1448. He attempted to sail up the Gambia River but was halted by warriors of the Mandinka tribe. Cadamosto made a second trip up the Gambia in 1456, stopping at the Cape Verde Islands along the way. This time, he was able to establish a peaceful understanding with the Mandinka through an interpreter. He then traveled sixty miles upriver. When he returned to Portugal, he brought Prince Henry an elephant tusk.

After a final attempt to conquer Tangier in 1458, Henry's health slowly began to fail. On one of the last voyages Henry sponsored, Pedro de Sintra reached Sierra Leone, which historians generally agree is the farthest point south reached by one of Henry's captains. In all the years of Prince Henry's single-minded obsession with exploring and charting the coast of western Africa, he never once accompanied any of his captains on a voyage. In spite of this, he remains one of the single greatest influences on European exploration. Historians later gave him the name by which we now know him: Prince Henry the Navigator.

This statue of Prince Henry the Navigator stands in New Bedford, Massachusetts.

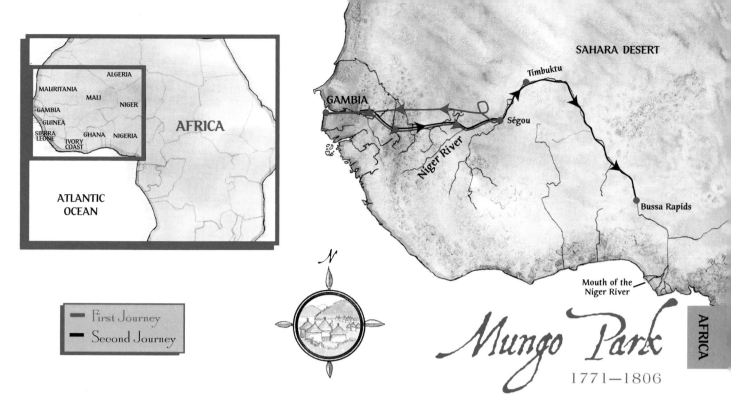

Mungo Park
1771—1806

First Journey
Second Journey

SAHARA DESERT

GAMBIA

Timbuktu

Ségou

Bussa Rapids

Niger River

Mouth of the Niger River

AFRICA

ATLANTIC OCEAN

ALGERIA

MAURITANIA

MALI

NIGER

GAMBIA

GUINEA

SIERRA LEONE

GHANA

IVORY COAST

NIGERIA

N

Tall and powerfully built, with milky skin and mesmerizing eyes, Scotsman Mungo Park looked every bit the part of the heroic explorer. Born in Selkirk, Scotland, to an upper-middle-class family, Park obtained his degree as a surgeon and then moved to London.

There he was introduced to Sir Joseph Banks, the highly influential creator of the Association for Promoting the Discovery of the Interior Parts of Africa. After Banks arranged for Park to travel to the East Indies, he decided that Park had all the qualities the association was looking for in an explorer. The association had previously sent an Irishman, Daniel Houghton, into Africa to search for the Niger River and locate Timbuktu. However, Houghton died of fever before he could return. Park was eager to have a try, and he began his journey in Gambia in June 1795, accompanied only by several slaves. His expedition was nearly halted by a local king with a reputation for not allowing traders to pass through his territory. But Park delighted the king with an umbrella, and the group was allowed to go on their way.

Park was not so lucky when he reached an area he called Benown (probably in present-day Mali) and was taken prisoner by a Muslim named Ali and his followers. The Muslims held Park prisoner for four months, unsure of what to do with him. They often neglected to feed him and kept him in a hut in scorching hot conditions. He began having trouble breathing and seeing. Finally Park saw a chance for escape one night in June 1796. Weakened by near starvation and illness, Park nevertheless forged toward the Niger River. He managed to reach it on July 20 and confirmed his previous theory that it ran from west to east. Too weak to continue exploring alone, he made his way back to London.

His return to England was a triumph. He published *Travels into the Interior District* in record time, and the first printing of the book sold out in less than two weeks. Now considered a hero, Park moved to Scotland to practice medicine and married Alice Anderson, daughter of a doctor he had studied with. But the quiet of country life eventually became too much for Park. When the association presented a plan to return him to Africa, he accepted it. This time the expedition was government-organized and would include thirty soldiers. Park was given the rank of captain, with orders to explore the Niger by boat.

In what is now considered a terrible mistake, Park and his men set out at the height of Africa's rainy season. Malaria and dysentery were rampant, and the men sickened one after the other. Of the approximately forty Europeans who had begun the expedition, only twelve reached the Niger River alive. By the time Park was ready to take a boat down the river, the number of survivors had dwindled to five. Among the last to die was his brother-in-law, Alexander Anderson.

Leaving only his guide onshore with instructions to send word to England of their situation, Park and his four companions built a canoe and headed down the Niger. They were never seen or heard from again.

Various theories circulated as to what

Engraving of Mungo Park

happened to Park. His guide was said to have heard that Park drowned in the Bussa Rapids. Other rumors held that he and his men engaged in a gunfight with hostile natives. Park's wife held out hope, but Park disappeared without a trace.

Sir Joseph Banks

Few explorers planned and funded their own expeditions. In the eighteenth century, one of the most influential and highly regarded sponsors of exploratory expeditions was Sir Joseph Banks. Born in London in 1743, he used his inheritance to further his scientific and social ambitions. As a member of the Royal Geographical Society, the most prestigious scientific organization in England, he had influence enough to secure himself a position on Captain Cook's first groundbreaking journey to explore the Pacific Ocean. Banks later went on to organize the Association for Promoting the Discovery of the Interior Parts of Africa. Its members were mostly wealthy, socially prominent, and dedicated to sponsoring expeditions that were largely scientific in nature. The association handpicked its "agents," as the explorers were called, negotiated salaries, determined itineraries, and was entitled to the exclusive receipt of all information gathered on the agents' excursions. Mungo Park's relationship with Banks opened doors for him—most importantly, the door to Africa.

Sir Joseph Banks

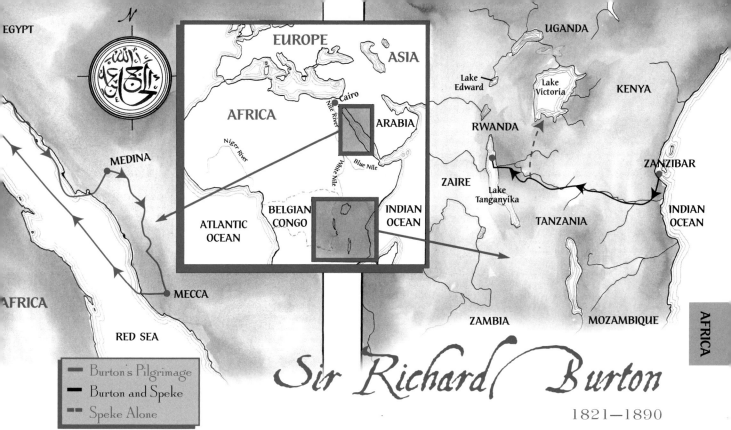

Sir Richard Burton

1821–1890

Though Richard Burton is often categorized as an explorer, his talents and abilities transcended any one field. He had a gift for languages, and he was an accomplished writer, translator, and ethnographer.

Richard Burton was born in Torquay, England, to an army officer who moved the family as many as fourteen times in ten years. Thus, Burton's education took place mostly at home, until he entered Oxford at the age of nineteen. He planned to fulfill his father's wish that he become a clergyman, but he became dissatisfied with the university and was expelled. He then entered the British Bombay Indian Army, where he taught himself Hindustani. He also added Persian, Sindhi, Punjabi, Armenian, and Turkish, among others, to the languages he had mastered. He began some of his first translations of Indian literary masterpieces, and by 1852, he had published four books of his own about India.

In 1853, during a leave of absence from the army, Burton shaved his head, grew a beard, and dyed his skin with walnut juice. With traditional Muslim clothes, his disguise was complete, and he traveled from Cairo, Egypt, to the Muslim holy city of Mecca. The prophet Muhammad had centuries earlier forbidden any non-Muslim to enter Mecca under penalty of death. But Burton was successful in remaining disguised during his visit. He also visited the holy city of Medina undetected.

He followed up this accomplishment by traveling to Harar (in present-day Ethiopia), also forbidden to outsiders, which no European had previously seen. But Burton and his companions, William Stroyan and John Hanning Speke, were attacked by Somalis. Stroyan died, and Burton and Speke were wounded.

Burton continued fulfilling his army duties by serving in the Crimean War, but he longed to return to Africa and explore the Nile. With the backing of the Royal Geographical Society, Burton and Speke

Engraving of Sir Richard Burton

departed for Zanzibar in June 1857 and from there headed inland to central Tanzania. Burton fell very ill with malaria during this time and for eleven months of the journey had to be carried on a makeshift stretcher. Speke was half blind due to an eye infection. They pressed on nonetheless, following rumors of an enormous "sea" nearby. In February 1858, they found four-hundred-mile-long Lake Tanganyika, the world's longest freshwater lake. On their return trip, Speke went alone to investigate the north of Tanganyika, leaving the ailing Burton behind. His actions would later be seen as the beginning of a long and tragic feud between the two explorers. When they returned to England, Speke alone visited the Royal Geographical Society to report his discoveries, something he had promised he would not do without Burton.

Burton took a break from exploration and visited the United States. When he returned to London, he married Isabel Arundell, over her mother's strong objection. English Victorian society deemed many of Burton's writings and their frank depiction of native customs unseemly. Despite this, Isabel was determined to marry Burton.

After the nuptials, Burton took several trips around Niger and the Gabon River and part of the Congo. Burton returned to his wife in England, where a large controversy began to brew over which of the explorers, Burton or Speke, was correct in his assessment of the Nile's source. Burton thought it was Lake Tanganyika, and Speke thought it was Lake Victoria. It became a bitter feud, with accusations and counteraccusations printed in the newspapers. A public debate was scheduled for September 1864, but Speke's death the day before the debate was to take place brought the feud to an end.

Sensing the need for a change, Isabel used her connections to secure Burton the British consulate in Brazil. Though he initially enjoyed his appointment, he eventually grew restless. Isabel secured him a consulate position in a place far more desirable to Burton: Damascus. Syria was at the time under the rule of the Turks, and Burton was eager to return to the land of deserts and leave the rain forest behind.

While in Damascus, Isabel wrote and published a book, *Inner Life of Syria*. The Burtons were happy in Damascus, but various trips and excursions often got them into trouble. On one trip to Nazareth, a beggar entered Isabel's tent as she slept. The beggar and Burton's servants came to blows, which escalated when more people became involved. The Burtons were also overly involved in local issues, including the baptism of a number of Muslims who were converting to Catholicism. Ultimately Burton lost the post of consul and returned to England. After a brief stint in Iceland exploring mining possibilities, Burton won the post of consul in Trieste in present-day Italy in 1872.

A baboon walks on the shores of Lake Tanganyika in Tanzania.

Weakened by years of suffering from tropical diseases, wounds, and physical hardship, Burton spent many of his final years writing books and translating works such as *The Arabian Nights* into English. At the time of his death in 1890, he was working on a translation of *The Scented Garden.* Disapproving of its controversial content, Isabel burned the almost completed translation, along with all of Burton's private diaries. Though scholars considered the loss of Burton's papers a tragedy, he did leave behind over fifty published works, both translations of Asian classics and original compositions.

The River Nile

The Nile, the world's longest river, captured the imaginations of nineteenth-century explorers just as the North and South Poles and the Northwest Passage did. The Nile, flowing through east and northeast Africa, is approximately 4,160 miles long and has been a source of life to the people of the Nile Basin for thousands of years.

Since ancient times, the source of this great river posed a puzzle to geographers and explorers. By the mid-nineteenth century, Western explorers and missionaries were beginning to slowly open Africa up to the outside world. The discovery of the source of the Nile was a significant goal that attracted some of the century's most notable explorers, including Richard Burton, John Hanning Speke, and Henry Morton Stanley.

By the end of the nineteenth century, following feuds and mysterious disappearances, it was determined that John Hanning Speke had been correct in identifying the source as Lake Victoria, the world's second-largest freshwater lake. Explorers turned their attention to other goals, and the Nile, winding and mysterious, continues to sustain life and travel throughout Africa.

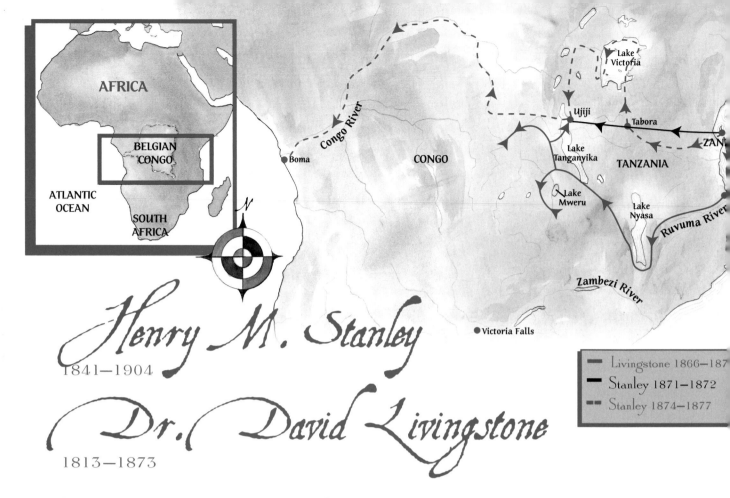

AFRICA

BELGIAN CONGO

ATLANTIC OCEAN

SOUTH AFRICA

Congo River

Boma

CONGO

Lake Victoria

Ujiji

Tabora

ZAN

Lake Tanganyika

TANZANIA

Lake Mweru

Lake Nyasa

Ruvuma River

Zambezi River

Victoria Falls

Henry M. Stanley
1841—1904

Dr. David Livingstone
1813—1873

Livingstone 1866—187
Stanley 1871—1872
Stanley 1874—1877

The brief partnership in Africa of Stanley and Livingstone produced one of the most famous utterances in the history of exploration: Stanley's deliberately casual, "Dr. Livingstone, I presume?"

Stanley and Livingstone began and ended their careers entirely separately. David Livingstone was born in Scotland to a poor family. By the age of ten, he was working in the local cotton mill, saving part of his meager salary to buy books. Largely self-educated, Livingstone saved enough money to enter school to study medicine. His dream was to become a physician and missionary and bring Christianity to the farthest reaches of the world. He joined a missionary society, which sent him to South Africa in 1841. There he met his future wife, Mary Moffat, daughter of a local missionary.

Livingstone continued his efforts to convert native Africans to Christianity and eventually established another mission even farther from civilization, in Koloberg. He

brought his family there with him. Increasingly interested in the pursuit of exploration, Livingstone began making trips to ever more remote regions of Africa's interior. He explored the Kalahari Desert, charted the Zambezi River, and discovered Victoria Falls. Livingstone was successful, but his family suffered. Mary, long weakened by enduring illnesses and pregnancies in the brutal jungle conditions, became sick and died in 1862. The children returned to England to live with Livingstone's mother.

As his fame as a missionary-explorer grew, the Royal Geographical Society encouraged Livingstone to continue his efforts in Africa. After returning to England for a period, Livingstone went back to Africa in 1865, one of his goals being to confirm the

Engraving of Dr. David Livingstone

source of the Nile River. A year later, the first rumors of his death began to circulate. Though letters with his signature appeared, proving he was alive, rumors of Livingstone's death continued to surface. It was then that the *New York Herald* decided Livingstone could be the story of the decade. They contacted reporter Henry Morton Stanley.

Stanley was born in Wales to an unmarried mother who could not raise him. She named him John Rowlands, after the man thought to be his father. By the time he was five, Stanley was a resident of a poorhouse, where the needy could sleep and eat in exchange for hard labor. At fifteen, Stanley escaped the poorhouse and found work on a ship crossing the Atlantic. Once in the United States, he sustained himself by working in a shop and then joined the Confederate army in 1862, the second year of the Civil War. He participated in the notoriously bloody battle of Shiloh and was later captured and sent to a military prison in St. Louis. Renouncing his loyalty to the Confederacy, Stanley then served in the Union army and gained his freedom. Eventually he found work as a newspaper reporter, now calling himself Henry Morton Stanley. He heard about a British expedition to Abyssinia and went along to cover it for the newspaper. The career of one of the great journalists of the Victorian age was launched. By the time the *New York Herald* assigned Stanley to go to Africa in search of Livingstone, the reporter was a seasoned traveler. But he had no experience leading expeditions himself, and certainly none as grueling as the march to Africa's interior.

Stanley outfitted his search expedition on the island of Zanzibar, off Africa's east coast. He brought with him several Africans who had traveled with other explorers. He also hired a great number of porters to carry supplies, which have been estimated at six tons. Stanley's group of 292 men left Zanzibar in March 1871 and headed into present-day Tanzania. His ultimate goal was to look for Livingstone at Lake Tanganyika and the village of Ujiji—740 miles into the African interior.

It was an exhausting and backbreaking journey over largely treeless ground. Temperatures could top 120 degrees Fahrenheit, and the men were vulnerable to diseases such as malaria, sleeping sickness, and dysentery. In an area called Tabora, Stanley became caught up in a war between a local bandit and a group of Arabs. This caused Stanley and his party to lose time traveling around the bandit's territory.

In October, tired, sick, and hungry, several of the men instigated a rebellion against Stanley. It almost resulted in a gunfight, but Stanley regained control without bloodshed. About one month later came the break Stanley had hoped for. Some Africans stopped to talk with Stanley and told him of a white man they had seen eight days earlier in Ujiji. Stanley was beside himself with excitement—he was convinced the white man had to be Livingstone.

Henry Morton Stanley stands with a group in Zanzibar.

Hearing that men were approaching Ujiji, Livingstone had come out of his hut and was standing among a group of people outside. Stanley came forward, noting to himself that the object of his search looked as frail and sickly as a very old man. He then extended his hand and asked the now-famous question, "Dr. Livingstone, I presume?"

Stanley had brought Livingstone much-needed supplies and medicine, and the men became friends in the ensuing months. But the idea that Stanley had "found" and rescued Livingstone is inaccurate. He was not lost at all. Although he was glad of Stanley's help, Livingstone only wished to remain doing what he was doing, traveling in Africa as an explorer and missionary.

When Stanley began his journey home, he took with him a box of letters from Livingstone. Although a variety of illnesses and old injuries were making him weaker and weaker, Dr. Livingstone would not leave Africa. After Stanley's departure, Livingstone spent another year exploring, still searching for the source of the Nile. On May 1, 1873, his servants found him dead on the floor. His remains were eventually returned to England and buried in Westminster Abbey.

Stanley returned to Africa in 1874 on assignment for his newspaper. He charted an enormous amount of territory along the Congo River. Belgium's King Leopold II later hired Stanley to acquire territory in the Congo area and establish a colony there. On his last trip to Africa in 1888, Stanley was sent to rescue the governor of the Equatoria province in Sudan, who was in the midst of a rebellion. By the time Stanley reached him, however, he was already safe.

When Stanley finally returned to England, he married and was elected to the House of Commons. He died in 1904 and is remembered along with Livingstone as one of the greatest explorers of Africa.

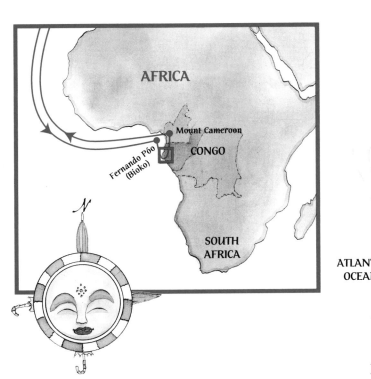

Mary Kingsley

1862—1900

Of all the explorers to lose their hearts to Africa, Mary Kingsley was truly notable. She was born in England, the daughter of a prominent doctor. She grew up in a house full of books, and two of her uncles were published writers. Though she received little formal schooling, Mary managed to educate herself thoroughly by reading in her father's library. She learned Latin and German and taught herself the basics of science. She was particularly interested in the works of African explorers Richard Burton and David Livingstone. However, in Victorian England a single woman's duty was to remain home and care for her parents' household. In 1892, Kingsley's parents both died. The following year she finally traveled to Africa, viewing the coast of the Congo area from Senegal to Angola and taking a two-month trip inland.

*I*t was in 1895, however, that Kingsley was able to truly experience Africa in the way that Livingstone and Burton had—by roughing it in areas few Europeans had visited before. She departed from Liverpool, reaching Sierra Leone in January 1895. Sailing south down Africa's western coast, she stopped at several major ports and visited with some friends on the island of Fernando Póo, which is present-day Bioko, off the coast of Cameroon. But her ultimate destination was the Ogooué River in Gabon, south of Cape Lopez. She intended to make her way as far up the river as possible, collecting fish specimens and learning everything she could about the local culture.

Once she arrived at the mouth of the Ogooué, she began her journey upriver on a small steamboat. She explored and collected her specimens by day, writing in her diary under mosquito netting in the evening. It was sometimes necessary for her to stop and deal with local officials bent on preventing her from continuing her dangerous trip. In spite of obstacles such as hippopotamuses,

Hippopotamuses have powerful enough jaws to bite right through a small boat.

Lambaréné, then began an overland journey toward Lake Ncovi. In spite of all advice to the contrary, she dressed in Victorian full-length skirts and petticoats. She insisted these garments were superior to pants, and her belief was borne out when she tumbled into a pit hidden in the ground and covered with pointed spikes. Kingsley's skirts were so thick that the spikes did not fully penetrate them. When her guide, thinking she must be dead, leaned into the hole and called down, "You kill?" she replied with her usual dry humor, "Not much."

On the last part of her journey through Gabon, Kingsley went from Esoon to Agonjo. In Esoon, she visited several rubber plantations, reaching one by wading through a swamp that left her covered with leeches. After spending some time in the area trading for items she needed and studying the customs of the local Fan tribe, she found a trader willing to take her down the Rembwe River and back to the coast. It was almost time to return to England, but Kingsley had one more adventure ahead of her.

Her journey would take her past Mount Cameroon, a volcanic mountain. At 13,353 feet, it is the highest mountain in West Africa's sub-Saharan territory. She cheerfully

crocodiles, violent rapids, and an angry local tribe, Kingsley was successful in ascending the Ogooué as far as Talagouga, where she fell out of a canoe and nearly drowned. Her manner in the face of these hardships was always cheerful. When Kingsley awoke one morning to a scorpion and two centipedes dropping onto her bed, she wryly wrote of her good fortune in not realizing they had been poised over her all evening.

She traveled back down the river as far as

Malaria

To the explorers of Africa during the Victorian age, malaria was a deadly foe. Malaria is caused by a microscopic parasite that invades a person's bloodstream when he or she is bitten by an infected mosquito. Initially malaria causes severe fever and chills and can ultimately cause death.

Though in Mary Kingsley's time it was not known how the disease was spread, it was known that the drug quinine could protect people from contracting it. But in remote regions of Africa, quinine often could not be obtained. Even today, malaria is still a deadly disease, killing over 1 million people per year.

approached the mountain with her porters in spite of the usual warnings and a heavy rain. Determined to continue in spite of rain-storms, a tornado, deserting porters, and missing supplies, Kingsley reached the summit of Mount Cameroon. She was the first woman to do so. With her usual sense of humor, she left one of her calling cards under a rock at the summit.

When Kingsley returned to England in late 1895, word of her travels was already widespread. She wrote a detailed and funny account of the trip, called *Travels in West Africa*. In addition to recounting her journey, she wrote about many of the customs and beliefs of the people she had visited, always with curiosity and respect.

Kingsley returned again to Africa in 1900, six months after the outbreak of the Boer War in South Africa. She nursed sick prisoners and soon contracted typhoid fever. Kingsley continued working until her strength left her completely. In June 1900, she died at the age of thirty-seven. Her writings remain some of the most popular works on Africa to this day.

The Boer War (1899–1902)

Europeans divided up parts of Africa among themselves, regardless of the people already living there. By the seventeenth century, a group of Dutch had colonized South Africa in the Cape Town area. As the settlement grew, the Dutch forced out the local Bantu people. In the nineteenth century, the British made their own claim to that land, annexed the territory, and established a British governor. They wanted to prohibit the Dutch Boers from continuing the slave trade. Under the new British government, power and control of the local gold mines largely passed from the Boers to the British. The Boers responded by refusing citizenship to the British and imposing high taxes to discourage them from staying.

Initially the Boers responded to British pressure and restrictive laws by relocating to an area in Africa's interior. In what is called the Great Trek, they moved in large groups to more remote areas of South Africa. But by 1886, gold had been discovered and the British were pouring into the area. In 1897, tensions peaked, and Britain, feeling it was protecting its commercial mining and territorial interests, began a war against the Boers.

The fighting commenced in October 1899 and continued until 1902, when the defeated Boers signed a treaty accepting British rule. Some 3,700 Boer lives had been lost, and peace would continue to elude the region.

Boer refugees, 1901

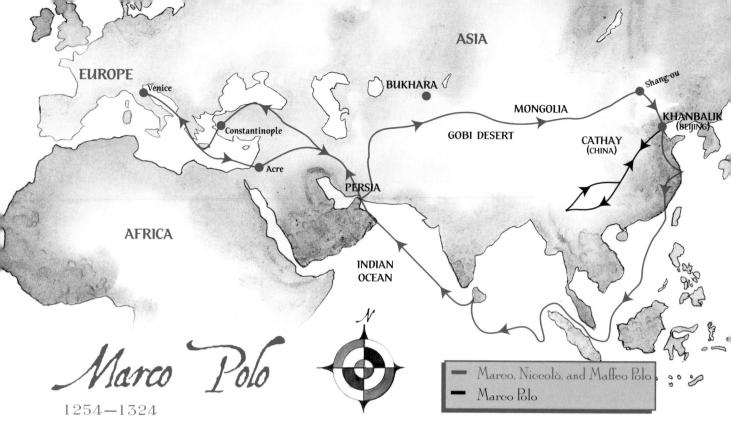

Marco Polo

1254–1324

The man often considered the world's greatest traveler was born in Venice to a family of merchants. Marco Polo's first fifteen years were spent without the company of his father, Niccolò Polo. Niccolò and his brother Maffeo had set out on a journey to find profitable places to trade jewels.

While in Bukhara (in present-day Uzbekistan), Niccolò and Maffeo devised a plan to join a diplomatic mission heading to the palace of Kublai Khan in Khanbalik. The great Mongol ruler was very pleased to have his first European visitors and asked them to take a message to the Pope inviting one hundred Christian scholars to teach him about Christianity and compare it with other religions. Kublai Khan also asked the Polo brothers to bring him oil from the lamp in Jerusalem's Holy Sepulchre. The Polo brothers returned to Venice in 1269. When they planned their second trip to visit Kublai Khan's court, they took seventeen-year-old Marco with them. They did not have the one hundred Christian scholars the khan had requested, but they did have two Christian missionaries and a letter from Pope Gregory X.

But the missionaries, cowed by the Mongols' reputation as fierce and brutal conquerors, lost their nerve and deserted the party.

The Polos' journey began in 1271 in Acre, in present-day Israel, where they obtained the Pope's blessing and received his letter and a gift of lamp oil for Kublai Khan. From Acre, the Polos probably followed caravan trails on the trade route called the Silk Road through southwest Asia to Persia and Afghanistan and, ultimately, central Asia. This final part of the journey was the most difficult. Known as the Flowing Sands, the Gobi Desert is plagued with severe winds that blow sand constantly and can easily turn a traveler in the wrong direction. The three Polos managed to stay on course, passing through the area of northern China then called Cathay before finally approaching Shang-ou, Kublai Khan's summer palace. The journey had taken them more than three years.

Kublai Khan was very pleased to see the three Polos and to accept the Pope's letter and gift. Marco Polo, in particular, made an extremely good impression on the Mongol ruler. Marco was an intelligent and curious young man who had an eye for detail, and he entertained the khan by recounting colorful stories of the people and places encountered on the journey. Always eager for information on neighboring peoples, Kublai Khan began sending Marco Polo on diplomatic missions throughout China and Tibet.

Marco Polo was equally impressed with Kublai Khan, declaring that his palace was "the greatest palace that ever was." He described the khan's luxuries at length, from golden walls to a stable of one hundred thousand horses. The palace had five gates, one used only by the khan. Marco could only estimate the number of bedchambers as "bewildering" and guessed that six thousand men could dine in the great hall. The palace was decorated with columns and marble walls and staircases, and in the khan's own chambers were heaps of treasure.

Marco Polo's first mission for the Great Khan was to a country he called Kara-Jang. By his own account, Polo completed his mission as instructed. His report to the khan was so lively and detailed that he was immediately sent on another mission. The Polos would remain with the Great Khan for seventeen years. During that time, Marco Polo, working as a diplomat and administrator, saw more of China and Tibet than any European before him. When the Polos finally wanted to return home, the Great Khan was not happy at the prospect of losing his European friends. He offered them immense wealth to make them stay. But the Polo men had grown weary of so much traveling and could think only of Venice. They were also aware that the khan had grown old. If he should die, they might

Mosaic of Marco Polo

not be able to return safely to Venice with all the wealth they had accumulated. They persisted in asking the Great Khan to let them go. Eventually their efforts paid off. When Kublai Khan suddenly had need of a trusted escort to bring a Mongol princess to her future husband in Persia, he turned to the Polos. They could go home, but only if they first brought the princess to Persia.

The journey by way of Persia to Venice took three years. When he finally arrived home, Marco Polo was a storehouse of information about the Far East. Although he wished to live quietly, Marco Polo was captured and taken prisoner in a war between Venice and Genoa. His cell mate was a writer named Rustichello. Listening to Polo's stories with fascination, Rustichello immediately saw the potential for a book. Polo sent for the notes he had taken during his many journeys, and the two men worked together to produce *The Travels of Marco Polo.*

Scholars have questioned how many of Polo's stories and claims are accurate, and several even wondered if Polo had been to China at all. The evidence is strong that much of his story is true. His book provided Europeans with their first real glimpse of Chinese and Mongol culture. It also gave historians a significant look at the lifestyle of Kublai Khan, one of the Mongol empire's greatest leaders.

We know little about Polo's life after the publication of his book. He married and had three daughters, and he died in Venice in 1324. Though many travelers followed in Polo's footsteps over the Silk Road across Asia, none recorded their journeys or published their stories except for the Muslim Ibn Battuta. By leaving us a detailed account of his experiences, Marco Polo ensured that his name and reputation as one of the world's greatest travelers would never be forgotten.

Kublai Khan and the Mongol Empire

Kublai Khan was forever immortalized in two great works of literature, Marco Polo's *The Travels of Marco Polo* and English poet Samuel Taylor Coleridge's "Kubla Khan." He was the grandson of the most famous Mongol conqueror, the ferocious Genghis Khan, who united the Mongols under his rule. The Mongol people originated in the area of east-central Asia now called Mongolia. Genghis Khan launched a campaign of warfare and conquest that encompassed most of Asia and penetrated into Europe. When he died in 1227, the empire was divided among four of his sons, who continued their own conquests in China, Russia, eastern Europe, Iraq, and Mesopotamia. When Kublai Khan came to power in 1259, he conquered southern China's Song empire and built his own capital at Beijing, which he called Khanbalik. The four Mongol kingdoms now reached from the Black Sea to the East China Sea.

Though a powerful and much-feared leader like his famous grandfather, Kublai Khan also possessed a tremendous intellectual curiosity. He believed that it was important to establish contact with the Christian world and was therefore pleased to receive the Polos.

Drawing of Kublai Khan and his soldiers

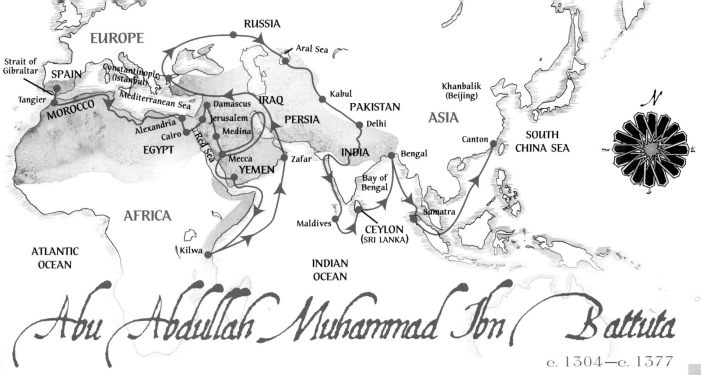

Abu Abdullah Muhammad Ibn Battuta

c. 1304–c. 1377

Marco Polo is often considered the world's greatest traveler, but in both number of countries visited and miles traveled, he is soundly beaten by the Arab known as Ibn Battuta. Like his Italian counterpart, Ibn Battuta left a magnificently detailed written account of his travels. No contemporary sources provide any information about his life, but Ibn Battuta's book tells us about his early years.

Born into a family of Muslim legal scholars, Ibn Battuta spent his childhood in the Moroccan city of Tangier, an ideal place to see traders and travelers. Tangier is a seaport on the northern coast of Africa, where the Strait of Gibraltar separates the continent from the Iberian Peninsula (modern-day Spain and Portugal) by as little as eight miles in the narrowest part. The Strait of Gibraltar provides the only sea route from the Atlantic Ocean to the Mediterranean Sea and served as a gateway for traders. Ships from Genoa and Venice frequently sailed west through the strait, then headed north toward England or south down the coast of West Africa. As he grew into a man in Tangier, Ibn Battuta would have seen a variety of cultures, Christian and Muslim alike, mingling in the seaport.

After several years of studying Muslim law, Ibn Battuta wished to make a pilgrimage to the Muslim holy city of Mecca, in present-day Saudi Arabia. It is the custom for all Muslims to make a journey of religious devotion, or pilgrimage, to Mecca at least once in their lives. Mecca is the birthplace of Muhammad, founder of Islam. In Ibn Battuta's time, pilgrims flocked there by the thousands to perform ceremonies of devotion and worship at the Great Mosque. From North Africa, a pilgrim could obtain passage partway across the Mediterranean on a ship and continue south on land. But the most popular route was to travel entirely overland, east along the northern coast of Africa and across Egypt and the Sinai Peninsula, then south across the Arabian Peninsula to Mecca. Because the journey presented many dangers to the pilgrims, including bandits, violent weather, and political hostilities, pilgrims often chose to travel in large groups called caravans.

Ibn Battuta set out from Morocco by himself to make his three-thousand-mile pilgrimage. In June 1325, he left his home in Tangier on a journey to Mecca that would ultimately take a year and a half. He traveled at a leisurely pace, stopping in the Egyptian cities of Alexandria and Cairo. He remained in Cairo for a month, enjoying the company of the busy city's most learned teachers and artists and praying at the local mosques. Then he followed the main road northeast to Damascus, taking short trips to Hebron and Jerusalem on the way. After arriving in Damascus, he spent three weeks attending lectures, visiting Damascus's

Ibn Battuta may have ridden part of his journey on camelback, like this modern-day traveler.

Great Mosque, and studying with local scholars. When a caravan of pilgrims departed Damascus for Mecca, Ibn Battuta joined them.

Ibn Battuta traveled with the caravan through Medina. Most pilgrims stopped at least briefly in this city, known as the City of the Apostle God. From there, it was two hundred miles to their final destination. Approximately seventeen months after leaving Tangier, Ibn Battuta arrived in the holy city of Mecca, where pilgrims from all over the Muslim world had come together to pray.

Unlike most pilgrims in the caravan, Ibn Battuta did not intend to return home the following month. He had seen some of the world outside Morocco, and he wanted to see much more. He traveled to Iraq and Persia (present-day Iran) with a caravan of Iraqi pilgrims, often exploring by himself, before finally returning to Mecca. He remained in Mecca for several years. He spent this time resuming his study of Muslim law, and he was now able

to earn money practicing law. But he did not remain in one place for long, and in 1328, he was on the move again.

He began a sea journey, sailing south through the Red Sea to Yemen and, from there, down the coast of East Africa as far as Kulwa, in present-day Tanzania. Then he sailed back to the Arabian Peninsula. His next major stop was Constantinople (now Istanbul), after which he visited the southern steppe lands of present-day Russia, then headed southeast past the Aral Sea as far south as Kabul in current Afghanistan. There he crossed into present-day Pakistan. Finally he reached Delhi in India. It was here that Ibn Battuta took a rare break, spending the next eight years in Delhi working for the sultan's court as a lawyer.

When the sultan asked Ibn Battuta to escort a party of Chinese diplomats back to their home, he agreed. The large party set out in several Chinese sailing vessels called junks. However, running into bad weather off the coast of India, the ships were driven aground and wrecked. Fearing the sultan's wrath, Ibn Battuta did not return to Delhi.

He continued with his restless movement, visiting the Maldives, islands off the southwest coast of India, then traveling to the island of Ceylon (now called Sri Lanka) in the Indian Ocean. In Bengal, he boarded a Chinese junk bound for Sumatra, an island off the Malay Peninsula, and there he obtained the use of another junk that brought him to China. After visiting Canton, Ibn Battuta seems to have had enough of traveling. His next move was in the direction of Mecca, and he revisited India, Persia, Arabia,

and Damascus on the way. When he arrived in Morocco in 1349, the young man who had left Tangier to make a pilgrimage to Mecca had been gone for twenty-four years.

His accomplishments had not gone unnoticed, and Morocco's sultan hired a writer to help Ibn Battuta record his incredible journey. Though he made one last trip, to Mali, he was for the most part content to remain in Morocco, which he declared was his favorite of all the many lands he had seen. Ibn Battuta died in Tangier around 1377. While his tomb is commonly believed to be in Tangier, the last resting place of the restless traveler may or may not contain his actual remains.

Pilgrimages to Mecca

For any devout follower of the Muslim faith, the pilgrimage to Mecca, called the hajj, is a profound and highly celebrated experience. One of the five pillars of Islam, the hajj has been a centerpiece of Muslim life for centuries, and every Muslim who is physically and financially able is required to perform it at least once. The hajj takes place each year in the twelfth month of the Islamic lunar calendar and lasts for five days.

Muslims travel in huge numbers to Mecca, the birthplace of the religion's founder, Muhammad. They wear special clothes and perform numerous prayers and rituals, including a ritual during which pilgrims walk seven times around a sacred stone called the Kaaba in Mecca's Great Mosque. They then pray at the Plain of Arafat, where Muhammad delivered his farewell sermon in AD 632.

Muslims who complete the pilgrimage believe that all sins committed during their lifetimes are now wiped clean. In modern times, it is estimated that up to two million Muslims make the pilgrimage annually.

Pilgrims in Mecca in the late 1800s

EUROPEAN CARAVEL   CHINESE TREASURE SHIP

Zheng He (also Cheng Ho)
c. 1371 — c. 1435

The fifteenth century was China's age of exploration, and there is no greater or more celebrated Chinese explorer than Admiral Zheng He. In twenty-eight years, Zheng He traveled to over thirty countries and was the emperor's most trusted advisor. But Zheng He began his life far from the emperor's palace.

He was born into a Muslim family and taken prisoner by the Chinese when he was a boy. He worked as a houseboy in the home of a Chinese prince, Zhu Di. When China's emperor died, the new emperor, Zhu Yunwen, began to eliminate his rivals and wanted to have the prince killed. Zhu Di left his home and hid in the streets, pretending to be insane and homeless. All the while, he was followed and protected by Zheng He.

Eventually Zhu Di was able to enlist supporters and gather an army to challenge the emperor. He was successful, and Zheng He was his most trusted ally and companion. Zhu Di became the new emperor and appointed Zheng He commander in chief of China's growing naval fleet. Determined to expand China's influence and power in the world, the emperor had new ships built at a rapid rate.

In 1405, the emperor sent Zheng He to Indochina on the first of seven voyages. By now, China's fleet was the largest and most powerful in the history of the world. When Zheng He departed, he had three hundred ships and twenty-eight thousand men under his command. The ships themselves were masterpieces—nothing like them existed in the rest of the world. The largest, known as treasure ships, were ten times the size of their European counterparts. Nine-masted, four hundred feet long, and four stories high, each treasure ship employed a crew of almost one thousand people. The mere sight of the fleet was awe-inspiring. In addition to their massive size, the ships were groundbreaking in their design. They were flat-bottomed and had central rudders and watertight bulkheads that could be sealed off in the event of a leak.

It was Emperor Zhu Di's goal to expand China's authority in every way. At great expense, he rebuilt the Great Wall, which had been crumbling for hundreds of years. He also employed over a million workers to build a new palace, the Forbidden City. The fleet was intended to carry out diplomatic missions—carrying priests, translators, and ambassadors—as well as those of exploration and trade. Over the course of his seven voyages, Zheng He took his fleet throughout Asia, Africa, the Middle East, and India. Some present-day scholars think that ships from the fleet may also have reached Australia, New Zealand, and even Central America seventy years before Christopher Columbus landed in the New World. But most records of their voyages, and ultimately most of the ships themselves, were blotted from China's history in the political upheaval that followed.

The Confucians, who were against trade and expansion, were gaining the upper hand in China and wanted the country to isolate itself and look to tradition. A series of misfortunes in China made the people wonder if their emperor had angered the gods by spending so much money and manpower to build and expand the country. A severe lightning storm that set fire to the emperor's palace seemed to confirm that the wrath of the gods had been invoked. More and more, public opinion began to turn against the emperor's building and spending and, specifically, against the resources invested in the powerful naval fleet.

After the death of the emperor in 1424, the struggle for power began in earnest, with the Confucians gradually winning out. One of Confucius's teachings specifically denounced the making of long voyages seeking profits.

The Great Wall of China

The Confucians ordered all ships to return to China and oversaw the destruction of all of Zheng He's maps and records. Authorities later outlawed the building of large ships and, in 1524, destroyed all ships capable of ocean crossings.

Zheng He died sometime around 1435. Although his tomb is in Nanjing, locals say it was dug up in 1962 and was empty. Little trace of Zheng He remains in China, though during the course of his life, he saw China change from the greatest and most influential sea power in the world to an isolated nation.

Court of the Imperial Palace, Forbidden City, Beijing

Confucius and Confucianism

The Chinese teacher and philosopher whose westernized name is Confucius (for K'ung Fu-tzu) was born in the present-day Shandong Province of China around the year 551 BC. His father was a military officer who provided a comfortable but not wealthy home. Confucius inherited his father's great height and imposing build, but his interests lay more in studying than in the military.

During Confucius's youth, there were frequent tensions and battles with neighboring Chinese states, encouraged by harsh and sometimes cruel rulers. Confucius began to formulate a philosophy that would come to be known as Confucianism. Largely concerned with morals and appropriate behavior, Confucianism stressed the link of each person by a common *jen,* or compassionate love for humanity, and defined a system of correct conduct for the various relationships in life, from father-son to ruler-ruled.

Students flocked to Confucius for instruction in his principles, and he enjoyed great popularity during his lifetime. When he died in his seventies, his students wrote down all that they could remember of his philosophy and his sayings. This collection is now known as *The Analects of Confucius,* and it has been studied and celebrated for more than two thousand years.

Over time, Confucius's teachings have gone from being officially celebrated to officially outlawed and back again. In the second century BC, all of his works were ordered destroyed by the rulers of the Ch'in Dynasty. But they were preserved, and later scholars studied and added to the ideas. In the twentieth century, the philosophy of Confucius was again attacked and dismissed as being backward and out of date. In the last several decades, however, public opinion has begun to shift once again, and the Chinese government now permits the study and pursuit of Confucian teachings and ideas.

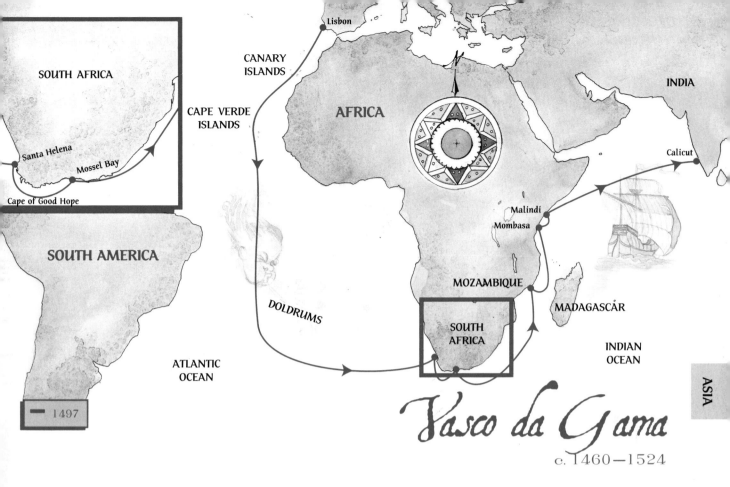

Vasco da Gama
c. 1460—1524

Within the span of one decade, the fortunes of Portugal turned as the nation suddenly became a major force of trade and exploration. In 1488, Bartolomeu Dias rounded the southern tip of the African continent, proving there was a sea route to the other side. By 1497, Vasco da Gama was ready to take Dias's discovery to the next level and follow the route until he found India.

Vasco da Gama was born in Portugal to a noble family of good standing. Da Gama followed in his father's footsteps as a naval commander, and his actions defending Portuguese colonies at Guinea from the French distinguished him in the eyes of the Crown. When Columbus returned successful from his 1492 voyage, the race to establish a sea route to India began to heat up. In 1494, the Pope established an imaginary line of demarcation around the globe. Spain was entitled to lay claim to all non-Christian lands it discovered to the west of the line. Portugal could claim non-Christian lands discovered to the east. This made Portugal eager to find an eastern route to Asia, particularly now that it was believed that Columbus had discovered the western route for Spain.

King Manuel I appointed Vasco da Gama to make the journey around the Cape of Good Hope and cross the Indian Ocean to reach the Indian subcontinent. He departed Lisbon on July 8, 1497, with four ships specially designed for the trip. Bartolomeu Dias accompanied the expedition for the first leg of the journey. Vasco da Gama's brother, Paulo, captained the *São Rafael*. Vasco himself traveled in the flagship, the *São Gabriel*.

As his small fleet sailed down the length of Africa's coast, Vasco da Gama departed

Watercolor painting of da Gama standing in the prow of a rowboat

from the course that Dias had taken a decade earlier. He instead took his ships significantly west, away from the coast. In this way, he avoided the Doldrums, the area of sea off the west coast of Africa known for its calm waters and shifting winds. When da Gama judged they were far enough south, the fleet approached the coast again. But his reckoning was off, and da Gama found he was still about three hundred miles from the tip of the African continent. Now in dangerous coastal waters where ships were often wrecked, da Gama proceeded cautiously south, stopping in present-day South Africa to make repairs to the ships. While collecting wood in the bay they named Santa Helena, da Gama's men encountered the native Hottentots (also called Khoikhoi) for the first time. Da Gama's men invited one of them on board and traded some goods, but their first exposure to the Hottentots ended unpleasantly. It is possible

that one of the Portuguese sailors accidentally offended the Hottentots in some way. Several men, including da Gama, were injured in an attack before the fleet could set sail.

They made landfall one last time, at Mossel Bay, remaining there for almost two weeks and acquiring meat and fresh water. As in Santa Helena, relations between the locals and the Portuguese began well but soured, and a fight broke out. Da Gama fired several of his cannons to show how powerful the Portuguese were, and the fleet sailed again.

The seas around the Cape of Good Hope were treacherous and stormy, but da Gama was an expert navigator. By December 10, the fleet had rounded the cape without damage. As they progressed farther into waters completely unknown to the Portuguese, the need to find a local pilot grew. Da Gama decided to make landfall in Mozambique and engage the services of two Muslim pilots by offering gold to the local sultan. The sultan accepted the gold but was suspicious of the Portuguese. Muslims controlled trade in this area of Africa, and they did not want Portuguese competition. One of the pilots resisted joining the fleet, and when the sultan denied da Gama access to a fresh water supply, violence broke out. Da Gama fired his cannons on the Muslims. When his fleet sailed from Mozambique, da Gama carried a number of Muslim prisoners on board.

Da Gama became increasingly violent. By the time the expedition reached Mombasa, the two Muslim pilots had escaped. Da Gama poured boiling oil on the skin of his prisoners to find out if a trap had been laid. In Malindi, da Gama again searched for a pilot who knew the waters between Africa and India. Some sources indicate that the pilot he found was a famous navigator named Ibn Majid, but his identity has never been proven. Whoever he was, the pilot led the Portuguese north along the coast and then east across the Indian Ocean. Twenty-three days later, they sighted land.

It had been ten months since leaving Portugal when da Gama and his small fleet arrived in Calicut, a city on India's western coast. Da Gama arranged for a visit with the local Hindu ruler, but he did not find favor. The gifts the Portuguese had brought were lackluster, consisting largely of cloth and clothing and some sugar and honey. The Hindu ruler was insulted that the Portuguese thought the Indians so simple as to be impressed by these meager gifts. Calicut was one of India's most important trading centers. Its citizens and merchants were accustomed to seeing Asia's most precious silks, jewels, and spices. Though there was no violence between them, the Portuguese and the Calicut natives were not off to a friendly beginning.

After a period of three months, da Gama and his men journeyed home to Portugal. Da Gama received a hero's welcome and was promptly made admiral of the Indian Ocean fleet. He returned to India several times to establish Portuguese trading posts, carrying a grudge against Muslims. He showed a brutal willingness to kill even women and children in order to make the Portuguese feared and obeyed. He was most ruthless with the city of Calicut itself, attacking and virtually destroying its port after an uprising against Portuguese settlers there. Through violence, he obtained the treaties and trade partnerships he sought and returned to Portugal with enormous wealth.

The Portuguese king appointed da Gama viceroy, or governor, of India and sent him there for the last time in 1524. Da Gama reached India but became ill and died there soon after. Though he was a cruel man who chose to rule by force, da Gama is nonetheless remembered as a pioneer whose eleven-thousand-mile voyage from Portugal to India changed the balance of power in Europe. Da Gama's journey is counted among the most important sea voyages in history.

The Legend of Prester John

The legend of Prester John and his hidden Christian kingdom intrigued and sometimes obsessed Europeans since it was first heard in the twelfth century. The first mention of Prester John (which means John the Priest) is found in the writings of a German bishop who had been told of a Christian monarch who ruled a vast kingdom somewhere in Asia or Abyssinia (present-day Ethiopia). Later in the twelfth century, a letter said to have been written by Prester John circulated throughout Europe. The letter described a kingdom overflowing with gold and jewels and completely devoid of any crime or sin whatsoever. The letter stated that seventy-two kings had accepted Prester John as their overlord, that his wealth was so great no one could calculate the value, and that he and his chosen subjects dined each night at tables made from emeralds.

The legend was so tantalizing that many of the great explorers of the time sought to locate the kingdom of Prester John. Vasco da Gama, Marco Polo, and Prince Henry of Portugal all hoped to find some trace of the legendary Christian monarch. None was ever successful. The letter itself is now considered a forgery. Whatever or whoever inspired the fanciful stories of a wealthy priest and his hidden kingdom remains a mystery.

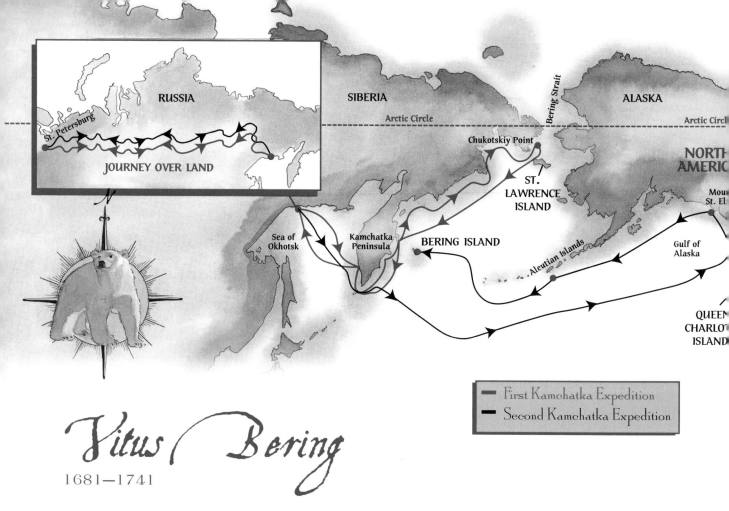

Map labels:
RUSSIA
SIBERIA
ALASKA
Arctic Circle
Arctic Circle
Bering Strait
Chukotskiy Point
St. Petersburg
JOURNEY OVER LAND
ST. LAWRENCE ISLAND
NORTH AMERICA
Mou St. El
Sea of Okhotsk
Kamchatka Peninsula
BERING ISLAND
Aleutian Islands
Gulf of Alaska
QUEEN CHARLOT ISLAND

First Kamchatka Expedition
Second Kamchatka Expedition

Vitus Bering

1681—1741

The Danish-born explorer Vitus Bering has left little trace of his childhood, and historians are not even sure if the few existing portraits of him are accurate.

Vitus Bering stepped into history in 1724 as a captain serving in the Russian navy. Russia was experiencing rapid growth in its naval power: shipbuilding was increasing, as was the study of navigation. Russia's czar, Peter the Great, felt it was time for Russia to organize some exploratory expeditions. Peter wanted to send a group of men to explore northern Siberia to find out who lived there, how much land there was, and if the territory had any mining potential. Most importantly, he wanted to know if there was a land connection to North America at Asia's easternmost point. Bering had sixteen years of experience sailing in the Arctic and Pacific waters, and Peter chose him to lead what is now called the First Kamchatka Expedition. When the czar died shortly after organizing

the expedition, he left strict instructions that his successor, Empress Catherine I, continue to support the efforts.

The task of getting the men and the lumber for ships across Russia to Siberia was staggering. Bering and his officers departed St. Petersburg in January 1725 and had to travel on foot, by dogsled, by riverboat, and on horseback over six thousand miles across Russia and Siberia to reach the Sea of Okhotsk on Siberia's eastern coast. They not only hauled many of their provisions for the next several years but also carried lumber and materials for shipbuilding. They were traveling to a largely unknown and sparsely populated region, and once they reached the Sea of Okhotsk, they would have to build their own seagoing vessel. Bering carried government authorization that permitted him to buy supplies and hire carpenters and soldiers along the way.

Crossing the snowy wastelands of Siberia took a heavy toll on the group. Several men died, more became ill, and some even deserted. Horses and dogs died of exhaustion. Bering's records show that of the 660 horses they set out with, only 393 survived to reach Okhotsk in October

Peter and Paul Fortress in St. Petersburg, Russia

1726. The journey had taken twenty-two months, and they still had a ship to build.

The carpenters began building a ship using the lumber they had hauled, as well as timber they cut down, but work was interrupted by the bitter Siberian winter. It was not until the following June that the ship was completed and ready to sail. Bering named her the *Fortuna*. While she took her first voyage into the Sea of Okhotsk, Bering's men built a second ship, the *St. Gabriel*. At last, Bering had prepared everything necessary to carry out Peter the Great's directions and sail northeast to determine whether Asia and North America were connected by land or separated by a strait of water. They sailed northeast along the coast of the Kamchatka Peninsula, stopping several times to talk to the local Chukchi people. However, the Chukchi did not have much geographical knowledge about the tip of the continent.

The most puzzling episode of the journey came in August 1728. Bering and the *St. Gabriel* had sailed as far as Cape Chukotsk, though the ship's log inaccurately calculated their precise position. In order to prove that a strait of water existed between the two continents, Bering should have continued sailing to the northeast long enough to sight North America to the north. But instead, Bering asked

his officers whether they felt they should continue or turn back. The officers provided their written opinions that they should continue sailing. Bering, however, decided to turn back.

It is thought that Bering believed he had discovered the strait, which now bears his name, based on what little information the Chukchi had given and his assumption that the coast of Siberia was falling off to the northwest. The *St. Gabriel* was technically in the Bering Strait when Bering gave the order to turn around. But it is difficult to explain why, after journeying three and a half years over six thousand miles, Bering would turn around after only fifty-one days at sea. He was just short of obtaining irrefutable visual proof that the strait existed.

Bering brought his ships back to the mouth of the Kamchatka River, and the party retraced their steps across Russia, reaching St. Petersburg in March 1730. Bering was criticized for not completing his journey by visually locating the North American coast. Nonetheless, the Admiralty College gave him a promotion and a raise. When a second expedition was organized, they again made Bering commander.

This Second Kamchatka Expedition, also called the Great Northern Expedition, was the largest scientific expedition in Russian history. Its goal was to further explore Siberia's Arctic coast. It included over one thousand members, including the first woman polar explorer, Maria Pronchishcheva. Bering had two ships built, the *St. Peter* and the *St. Paul*. His section of the expedition returned to the coast of Siberia, where he located and charted the Aleutian Islands, entered the Gulf of Alaska, and sighted eighteen-thousand-foot Mount St. Elias in Alaska. On the return voyage from Alaska, Bering's ship was separated from the *St. Paul* during a storm and was wrecked on an island now called Bering Island, one hundred miles east of the Kamchatka Peninsula. Bering and his men had to spend a bitter winter on the island, living in holes they dug in the sand. On December 8, 1741, Bering died of scurvy, as would nineteen members of his crew. The survivors built a new boat to take them home, finally reaching Kamchatka in August 1742.

In 1991, Danish archaeologists located Bering's burial site on Bering Island and transported his remains to Moscow, where his identity was confirmed. The following year, Bering was laid to rest permanently on Bering Island.

Semen Dezhnev and the Bering Strait

Contemporary Russian naval historian Evgenii G. Kushnarev begins his account of Bering's First Kamchatka Expedition by writing, "In our time, every Russian schoolchild knows that Asia and America are separated by a strait that was discovered by Semen Dezhnev in 1648." If this is so, why did Peter the Great send an expedition eighty years later to investigate the existence of a strait, and why is Bering so often credited with its discovery? Because Dezhnev's journey went mostly unrecorded in official government documents; a generation later, it had been forgotten almost entirely.

Dezhnev was born sometime around 1605, traveled extensively throughout northern Siberia and the territory of the Chukchi, and ultimately sailed through the strait separating Asia from North America. In spite of his accomplishments, many maps of the time did not include his discoveries, and no official government evaluation was ever recorded. By the time Peter the Great became interested in exploring Kamchatka, the fact that Dezhnev had discovered and sailed through the strait between the continents had been more or less forgotten.

Scholars have found plenty of documentation to establish acceptable proof that Dezhnev sailed through the Bering Strait in 1648. It is ironic that the man often credited with the strait's discovery, Vitus Bering, never actually sailed through it at all.

Cape Dezhnev and the Bering Strait

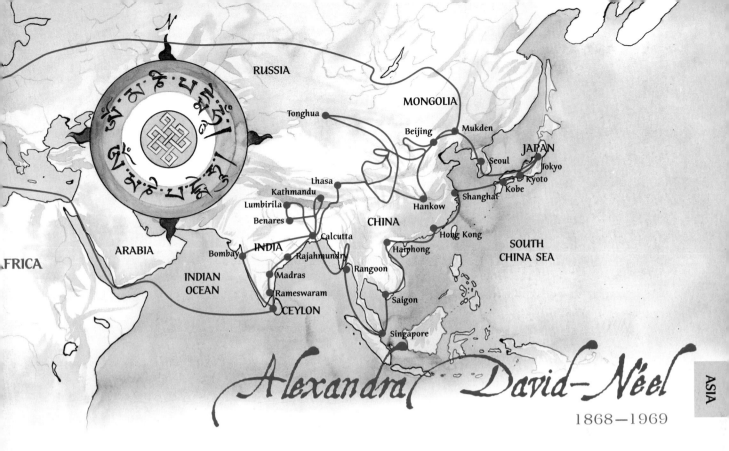

Alexandra David-Néel

1868—1969

Born near Paris in 1868, Alexandra David was a solemn girl who preferred reading, exploring, and climbing trees to dressing in fine gowns and fussing over her appearance. By the age of seven, she was already a zealous reader, favoring novels that introduced her to remote and exotic landscapes. Abandoning her studies and governess to go climb trees, Alexandra was already daydreaming of a wild land of mountains and glaciers. In her later years, she would come to know the land by its name: Tibet.

𝒰nwilling to remain within the confines of proper Parisian society, the adult Alexandra made her living as an opera singer. This occupation helped her satisfy her thirst for travel and privately pursue one of her passions, the study of Buddhism and the Sanskrit language. Exotic subjects at the time, they were particularly off-limits to women. Alexandra nonetheless found people and books to learn from. French businessman Philip Néel proved willing to indulge his wife's growing obsession with the Far East, offering to finance a yearlong trip throughout India. David-Néel eagerly accepted her husband's offer, and her planned one-year trip to India turned into a journey of almost fourteen years.

David-Néel traveled throughout Asia, including India, Ceylon, Sikkim, Nepal, Burma, French Indochina, Japan, Korea, and China. Almost everywhere David-Néel traveled, she was received with a level of respect and honor unheard of for a Westerner, let alone a woman. She became the first woman to be received by the thirteenth Dalai Lama, Tibetan Buddhism's highest and most revered figure. But David-Néel's greatest dream was to travel into Tibet itself, journey to its holy city of Lhasa, and see the golden-roofed Potala Palace with her own eyes.

By 1923, along with her faithful Sikkimese companion, Yongden, David-Néel was ready to attempt to cross the Chinese border

Alexandra David-Néel dressed
as a Tibetan nun

into Tibet. It was an extremely ambitious plan. During this time, Tibet was strictly off-limits to all foreigners. Nestled beyond the mighty Himalayan mountain range in central Asia, Tibet shares borders with China, India, and Nepal. Its lofty position, surrounded by mountains on all but one side, allowed the country to remain undisturbed by the outside world for hundreds of years. But as the nineteenth century ended, things began to change. Both Britain and Russia were keenly interested in Tibet. The little country would be an important addition to either empire. The Manchu emperors of China also saw Tibet as a great prize and considered the territory their own. Fearful of the hungry empires encroaching from all sides, Tibet closed its borders to foreigners. But David-Néel was not so easily stopped.

A petite, fifty-four-year-old woman, David-Néel set off in the dead of winter for Lhasa with little but the clothes on her back and a pistol strapped under her skirt. She rubbed soot into her face and dyed her hair black with Chinese ink so she would more closely resemble a Tibetan woman. She had spent years carefully mastering the Tibetan language and had lost the last traces of her French accent. When David-Néel stepped

across the border from China into Tibet in October 1923, she left behind all traces of her old identity and all the protection it might provide. She became an anonymous Tibetan peasant woman on a holy pilgrimage to Lhasa. She was in constant danger of being discovered as she was questioned by soldiers and government officials at the frequent checkpoints.

With Yongden, she walked through bandit-infested regions, avoiding soldiers, leopards, and roving gunmen. She was visited by visions, stranded in a rickety basket over a river, and welcomed into remote villages as a sorceress. Some foretold her coming; others spread stories of her miraculous powers. In spite of illness and lack of food and water, she remained on the move, crossing two mountain passes in a blizzard and taking refuge from the snow in a tiny cave. Four months after leaving China, Yongden and David-Néel caught sight of the glittering golden roofs of Potala Palace in the distance. Her arrival in the holy city of Lhasa was a triumph in many ways. In addition to realizing her most cherished dream, she had done what no European woman and only a handful of European men had ever accomplished—she had reached the heart of Tibet.

David-Néel remained in Lhasa for two months before returning to France. She was instantly famous for her accomplishments. The rest of her considerably long life was devoted to the pursuit, study, and protection of Tibetan Buddhism. She would eventually publish forty books on the subjects of Asian culture, Buddhism, and her travels. She provided priceless translations of ancient Tibetan manuscripts, material that in its original form was largely destroyed in later years by the Chinese. Her personal experiences with the mysterious rituals of Tibetan Buddhism and of Dalai Lamas past and present are a rare glimpse into a world that no longer exists in its entirety. David-Néel was also an accomplished photographer, and her surviving photographs of her travels throughout Asia preserve vital cultural records.

In her later years, David-Néel settled in her own miniature Tibet, a hillside dwelling in France called Samten Dzong that contained her collection of rare Tibetan books and artifacts. People from all over the world came to see her, seek her guidance, study or live with her, or simply sit at her feet. She died, still curious and eager to travel, one month short of her 101st birthday.

Buddhist Tibet

Sometimes called the Rooftop of the World, Tibet remained alone and isolated for centuries, nestled safely in the high Himalayas. Life for Tibetans changed little throughout the ages, and this was the way they wanted it.

Since the eighth century, Tibet has been a Buddhist country. Tibetan Buddhism is based on the Mahayana school, stressing a great reverence and compassion for all life and a belief that each person can live according to Buddha's teachings and find truth for him- or herself. Buddhists also believe in karma, in which good or bad actions affect later lives and the overall progress toward enlightenment, or nirvana.

Over the centuries, a huge number of monasteries were built in Tibet, home to more than a quarter of Tibet's male population. Other Tibetans farmed or traded for a living. In a vast country supporting relatively few people, Tibetans developed their reputation for being independent and free-spirited. The heart of Tibetan spiritual life was the holy city of Lhasa, the center for religious celebrations and festivals and the location of magnificent Potala Palace, home to the Tibetans' spiritual leader, the Dalai Lama.

In October 1950, eighty thousand Chinese troops marched into Tibet, marking the end of Tibetan isolation. Well over one million Tibetans were killed or allowed to die in prison. Of over a half million Buddhist monks and nuns, barely more than ten thousand survived. Most of the monasteries and universities were reduced to rubble. A large part of the communist Chinese plan to take over Tibet was to eliminate its religion by force. For nine years, the Dalai Lama remained in Lhasa, trying desperately to keep some kind of peace with the Chinese authorities. But as the symbolic leader of the Tibetan people and the living representation of Buddhism, the Dalai Lama was too great a threat to the Chinese. With his safety in increasing danger, the Dalai Lama fled with a small party, traveling on horseback and yak to the safety of India.

A half century later, still waiting to return to his beloved homeland, the Dalai Lama continues to work for peace.

Potala Palace in Lhasa, Tibet

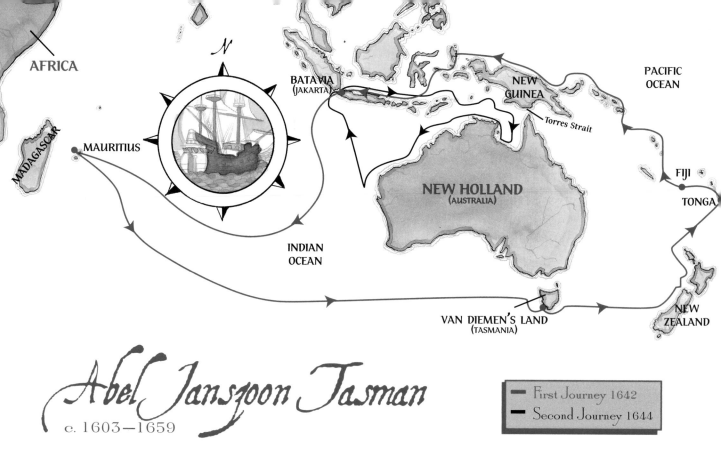

AFRICA

MADAGASCAR

MAURITIUS

N

BATAVIA
(JAKARTA)

NEW
GUINEA

PACIFIC
OCEAN

Torres Strait

INDIAN
OCEAN

NEW HOLLAND
(AUSTRALIA)

FIJI

TONGA

VAN DIEMEN'S LAND
(TASMANIA)

NEW
ZEALAND

First Journey 1642
Second Journey 1644

Abel Janszoon Tasman
c. 1603—1659

Though his superiors expressed disappointment with the career of Abel Tasman, the explorer is now recognized as having made a series of significant discoveries in the Pacific that would not be surpassed until Captain Cook took to the sea over a century later.

Abel Tasman was born in the Groningen province of Holland to a relatively poor family. Going to sea always offered prospects for a man who had little money of his own, and Tasman joined the Dutch East India Company in 1632. Here he gained valuable experience, sailing as far as Japan.

Beginning in the late sixteenth century, the Dutch had become an influential nation on the sea. The first Dutch voyage to the east was led by Cornelius Houtman in 1594 and went as far as the island of Java. By the time Abel Tasman commanded his own expedition in 1642, the Dutch had made several land-falls on the continent they called New Holland, which we know today as Australia. Dutchman Willmen Jantsjoon is said to have made the first landfall there in 1606, but it is

entirely possible a previous landfall went undocumented.

Tasman was given his first command by the governor-general of the Dutch West Indies, Anthony van Diemen, who was a motivating force behind the Dutch exploration of the Pacific. Van Diemen's orders were numerous—Tasman was to explore the Pacific, particu-larly the southern route to South America, identify the areas of New Holland the Dutch had previously seen, and search for evidence as to whether it was connected to Antarctica. Tasman's two ships sailed west from Batavia (present-day Jakarta in Indonesia) in August 1642. After refitting at the Dutch-occupied island of Mauritius in the Indian Ocean, Tasman and his two ships sailed south and then turned east into the prevailing westerly winds and currents, which would sweep them along.

By late November, they sighted a mountainous land in the distance. Unsure whether they were seeing New Holland or another landmass, they made for the land's west coast. Tasman named it Van Diemen's Land after the governor-general, but it eventually became known as Tasmania. Tasman explored the area's smaller islands, charting and naming them and producing maps of Tasmania's coastline. Eventually a party was sent ashore. Though they saw signs of habitation, no people appeared. A second party was sent ashore the following day to plant a flag and claim the land in the name of the Dutch republic.

Tasman took his ships east, and by mid-December, they had sighted yet another new land. Tasman and his men were the first Europeans to see this country, which would eventually be called New Zealand. Tasman incorrectly believed this land to be part of Staten Landt, an area off the coast of Tierra del Fuego in South America. When a canoe was launched from the shore, Tasman sent one of his own launches to meet it. The occupants of the canoe became suddenly aggressive, attacking and killing four of the crewmen with clubs. The remaining three escaped by swimming back to the ship. Tasman named the place Murderer's Bay and sailed off.

Tasman and his crew sailed around the north cape of New Zealand and continued east in search of the Solomon Islands. They did not find them but explored Tonga and Fiji instead. Tasman returned to Batavia on June 15, 1643. He had circumnavigated New Holland, but at too great a distance to chart the coastline. However, he did prove that New Holland was not connected to Antarctica. But Van Diemen was disappointed with Tasman's accomplishments, feeling he had not followed through on his discoveries. For example, Tasman did not determine whether the landmasses of present-day New Guinea and Australia were connected.

The Tasmanian Devil

Though Abel Tasman may not be a household name, almost everyone has heard of the Tasmanian devil. Now popularized as a Warner Brothers cartoon character, the real Tasmanian devil is a meat-eating marsupial. Because of its black color, sharp teeth, aggressive temperament, and terrifying screeches, Tasmania's early settlers called it a devil.

Measuring approximately two feet long and weighing up to twenty-six pounds, the Tasmanian devil is a nocturnal climbing mammal that lives primarily on rabbits, fish, and small reptiles. Thought once to flourish on the Australian continent, the Tasmanian devil is now extinct everywhere except the island from which it takes its name.

Tasman family

Guinea in February. Not seeing the Torres Strait separating New Guinea from New Holland, Tasman wrongly concluded the two were part of the same land-mass. Though he was able to make many more observations about New Holland's coastline before returning, the journal of the voyage was eventually lost, and only the charts re-mained. The charts pro-vided highly accurate and previously un-known information about the coastline of New

Nonetheless, Tasman was sent on a sec-ond expedition in 1644, this time with three ships. His orders were to take his 111-man crew to further investigate the relationship of New Guinea to New Holland and Van Diemen's Land. Tasman proceeded to New

Holland, but Van Diemen was once again dis-appointed with what he felt was a failed opportunity on Tasman's part. Tasman spent the rest of his life working as a merchant in Batavia. After the 1644 journey, he made no more expeditions of discovery.

The Last of the Hidden Tribes?

By the beginning of the twentieth century, there were few major land mysteries still unsolved by explorers, with the notable exception of Antarctica. But there were still undiscovered peoples.

In the early 1930s, Australian prospector Michael Leahy made a trip to the interior highlands of New Guinea to search for gold. There he came into contact with a tribe that was completely isolated. They did not know that an outside world filled with other people even existed. The Chimbu people, one of the tribes Leahy encountered, believed that their skin would turn white after death. When they saw these white-skinned strangers, they thought the spirits of their dead ancestors were returning.

Leahy took scores of photographs of the first encounters with the astonished and sometimes ter-rified natives. The pictures, used in a book and documentary on the subject, are an extraordinary testimony to the ancient, undisturbed world coming suddenly face to face with the modern world.

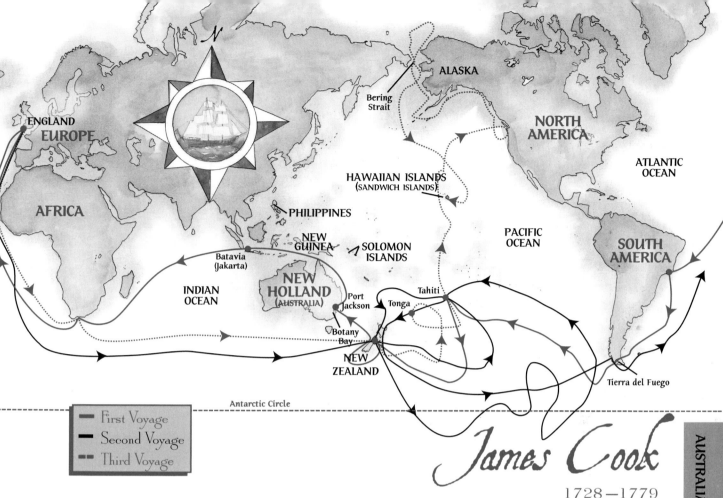

First Voyage
Second Voyage
Third Voyage

James Cook

1728—1779

James Cook was born in North Yorkshire, England, into fairly humble circumstances. It was unlikely that the son of a farm laborer could rise to become one of the British navy's brightest stars. But that was exactly what happened for James Cook.

As a boy, James Cook obtained very little formal schooling, but he was able to educate himself by reading. Cook was apprenticed to a shopkeeper, but he knew early on that the sea was his calling. A shipyard in Whitby gave him a three-year apprenticeship, after which he joined the British navy.

Cook's intelligence immediately caught the attention of his captain, Hugh Palliser, and Cook was soon promoted to master's mate. He proved good at learning the techniques of navigation and surveying. By 1757, he had passed his master's examinations. During the Seven Years' War, Cook continued to prove himself an exceptional sailor. After Cook had charted part of Canada's St.

Lawrence River and composed accurate charts of Newfoundland, his reputation as a skilled surveyor and navigator was well known.

In 1768, Cook was given command of the *Endeavor*. His orders were to take scientists and astronomers to the South Pacific to observe the transit of Venus, the moment at which that planet would pass between the sun and earth. The orders also included further exploration of the Pacific and New Zealand and the search for a southern polar continent.

The expedition sailed from England in August 1768. Stopping briefly in Brazil, it then passed through Le Maire Strait into the Pacific Ocean. In June, Cook reached Tahiti, which Samuel Wallis had discovered several

Captain James Cook

landmass. While there, Cook and his men had several encounters with the local Maori, who were largely hostile to outsiders. With his directive of nonviolence, Cook was mostly able to keep the peace.

Cook's next destination was the continent of New Holland, present-day Australia. Abel Tasman had charted some of the continent's coastline, but Cook set to work filling in the gaps. Among Cook's discoveries were Botany Bay and Port Jackson. Cook took possession of the Port Jackson area in the name of the British and named it New South Wales. Cook was also able to succeed where Tasman had failed: he proved that New Guinea was a separate island, not connected to New Holland.

Now sailing west, a number of the crew fell ill with dysentery and malaria. By the time Cook stopped in Batavia (present-day Jakarta), many were seriously ill and seven had died. The crew finally reached home on December 6, 1771. They had been gone over two and a half years.

years earlier. While on Tahiti, Cook ordered his men to treat the locals with the utmost respect. His attitude toward indigenous peoples would become a hallmark of his character for most of his career.

After leaving Tahiti, Cook headed south to search for the southern polar continent. He sailed south as far as his instructions had detailed but made no sight of land. Cook turned the ship around and headed for one of the lands Abel Tasman had discovered a century earlier, New Zealand. For six months, Cook and his men surveyed and made charts of New Zealand's coast. Cook proved that New Zealand was not connected to any other

Due to the success of the expedition, the British navy sent Cook on a second voyage almost immediately. Promoted to commander, he was given two ships, the *Resolution* and the *Adventure,* the second to be captained by Tobias Furneaux. On June 21, 1772, Cook began his second voyage. He headed south past the tip of South Africa, and by January 17, 1773, his ships had crossed the Antarctic Circle. The fog was thick, and *Resolution* and *Adventure* became separated. As previously agreed, the two ships rendezvoused in New Zealand.

Next they were to proceed east across the Pacific and head for Tahiti before returning to New Zealand. During this time, the ships were again separated and missed each other at the New Zealand rendezvous point. Cook took his ship south again for another attempt to find the southern continent, while Furneaux, arriving some weeks later in New Zealand, decided to return home. Before Furneaux left, eleven of his men who had gone ashore were killed by the New Zealand Maori.

Meanwhile, on board the *Resolution,* Cook had sailed to the farthest southern position ever reached. When he could go no farther because of the ice, he turned back, going first to the Tonga Islands and then to New Zealand. There he heard stories from locals of a deadly skirmish with white men, and he suspected crewmen of the *Adventure* had been involved. Crossing half the world yet again, Cook charted the coast of Tierra del Fuego and made one final push to locate the southern continent before heading home.

Again the British navy considered Cook's expedition a huge success. Cook was promoted to post captain and elected to the Royal Geographical Society. He temporarily took a post at the naval hospital at Greenwich, which gave him an opportunity to spend some rare time at home with his wife and children. Cook's wife, Elizabeth, would outlive every one of her six children, as well as her husband.

When the navy began planning a third voyage, Cook volunteered to command it. He was given two ships, the *Resolution* and the *Discovery* (to be captained by Charles Clerke). His orders were to explore the Pacific Northwest as well as to return Omai, a man who had accompanied them from the Society Islands, to Polynesia. After returning Omai, Cook proceeded north and discovered an entirely new group of islands, which he called the Sandwich Islands. Today they are collectively known as Hawaii.

On this third voyage, the men noticed a change in Captain Cook. Previously even-

tempered and fair, he was now often short-tempered, exhausted, and prone to rash fits of anger against both his men and islanders. He did not seem to be in any hurry to fulfill his orders, lingering at Tonga and Tahiti before proceeding to America's northwest coast. The ships reached the Bering Strait in August 1778. By September, they were returning south, toward the Hawaiian Islands. The ships landed on the island of Maui, unaware that their presence was fulfilling a local prophecy of the coming of the Hawaiian god Orono. Some historians think that the Hawaiians believed that Cook was the god.

The two ships' crews remained at Maui for over two months, during which time the Hawaiians showered them with gifts intended for Orono. Then the Hawaiians made it clear that it was time for the god and his ships to leave. *Resolution* and *Discovery* departed but only six days later sustained serious damage

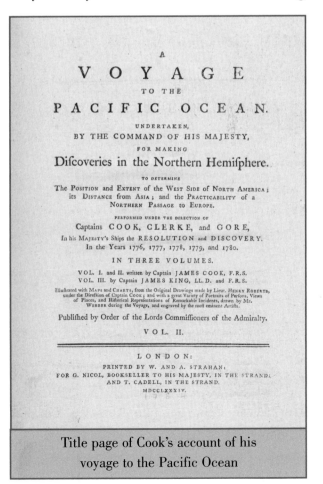

Title page of Cook's account of his voyage to the Pacific Ocean

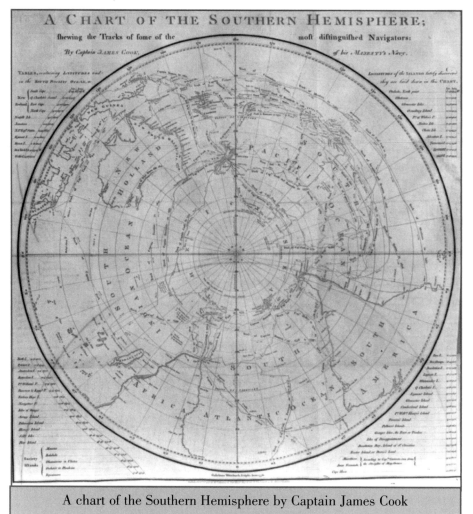

A chart of the Southern Hemisphere by Captain James Cook

pleased to see the two ships return. Cook was increasingly volatile. When a theft occurred, Cook responded with violence to the natives, even after the items were returned. The hostilities escalated. Cook was set on getting revenge for the theft and began firing on the natives and their homes. He went ashore with a group of men, intending to bring Hawaii's king on board as a hostage. The locals attacked the Englishmen, killing them all. Cook was the last to die as the rest of his men watched helplessly from their ship.

James Cook was mourned as a great captain and explorer and still ranks as one of the most accomplished officers of the British navy. As to his change in

in a storm. They had a choice: to keep going to the next island or return to Maui. Cook chose the latter, which would ultimately result in his death.

The Hawaiians were confused and dis-

personality during his last voyage, modern doctors have guessed that he picked up a progressive and serious stomach parasite, causing severe loss of nutrition and sleep and ultimately creating a mental imbalance.

Hygiene

A trait that set Cook apart from most other naval officers was his strict supervision of his men's diet and hygiene. Cook required the men to regularly bathe, launder their clothes, clean the ship, and eat foods rich in vitamin C. Though some of the men found these requirements irritating, Cook's crews had very few cases of scurvy or diseases caused by lack of cleanliness. His methods were copied widely in later years.

Jean-François de Galaup, Comte de la Pérouse

1741–c. 1788

Cape Horn

Rear Admiral Jean-François de Galaup, Comte de la Pérouse, is one of France's greatest Pacific explorers. But some historians feel that he has been so outshone by the famous Captain James Cook that he runs the risk of being forgotten altogether.

La Pérouse was born in southern France in 1741 and joined the navy when he was fifteen years old. He had an active and accomplished military career, particularly fighting against the English in the Seven Years' War and battles related to the American Revolution. When peace finally came in 1783, France's King Louis XVI decided it was time to dedicate some effort to a scientific exploration. The voyage was intended to explore the Pacific and the American Northwest. The expedition would establish new trade, study native peoples, and learn more about fur and whaling opportunities. La Pérouse was appointed commander of the expedition.

He departed France with his two ships, *L'Astrolabe* and *La Boussole*, to follow in the route of James Cook and fill in the gaps that the explorer had left in his expeditions. La Pérouse commanded *La Boussole*, and Captain Paul-Antoine de Langle commanded *L'Astrolabe*. After crossing the Atlantic and stopping in Brazil, the ships rounded Cape Horn, sailed along the coast of Chile, then made for Easter Island in the South Pacific, about two thousand miles off Chile's coast. Easter Island, already inhabited, had first been visited by the Dutch in 1722 and also by Captain Cook.

La Pérouse set up a small camp there,

Engraving of Jean-François de Galaup, Comte de la Pérouse

Sailing south, the expedition stopped in present-day Monterey, California, before proceeding west across the vast Pacific Ocean. In January 1787, they reached the island of Macao, forty miles west of Hong Kong, where they obtained new supplies before sailing for Manila and ultimately the Sea of Japan. La Pérouse surveyed Korea's coast, then worked his way north, providing the first accurate European charts of some areas of the Asian coast. They stopped to observe the island of Cheju, once home to a group of shipwrecked Dutch sailors for eighteen years. The ships reached their northernmost point in Kamchatka, in northeast Russia, before receiving new orders to proceed to Australia.

Their course took them by the Samoan islands, where they met with their first serious bloodshed. *L'Astrolabe*'s captain, de Langle, went ashore with a group of men to collect fresh water. A large group of Samoans gathered to observe them. For reasons that remain unclear, the Samoans attacked. De Langle and eleven of his men were killed. La Pérouse decided not to retaliate, instead sail-

undertaking a survey of the island and its people that took less than a full day to complete. The men collected information on the island's residents, investigated their crops, and visited the enormous carved heads for which the island is still known. Often dismissive of native peoples, La Pérouse declared the famous carvings only showed how backward the locals were in the art of sculpture. However, he did admit to being baffled as to how the heavy stones could possibly have been raised into place.

After leaving Easter Island, the ships made for the island of Maui, in Hawaii, where La Pérouse again went ashore long enough to examine and report on the customs of the local people. Then he set a course north, toward the coast of present-day Alaska. The expedition collected significant scientific and geographical information in this area and came away convinced that there was no navigable northwest passage there.

Eighteenth-century French medal commemorating Jean-François de Galaup, Comte de la Pérouse

ing for Tonga. From there, his course was southwest to Australia and Botany Bay.

It is known that La Pérouse and his two ships arrived safely in Botany Bay in January 1788 because he sent letters from that port reporting on the expedition's findings to date. After those letters were sent, La Pérouse was never heard from again, nor was there any hint of what became of his ships and crew. The French National Assembly sent a search expedition in 1791, but no trace of the missing party was found.

It was not until 1826 that English captain Peter Dillon heard rumors of two European ships that had been wrecked on the reefs off the island of Vanikoro, in the Solomon Islands. It was generally accepted—based on wreckage found and reports from the island's inhabitants—that the two ships had been wrecked on the reef off the coast. Some of the survivors were said to have been killed by islanders, and others to have made peace and lived there until they became old men. A third vessel was said to have been built by some of the survivors, who were thought to have set out west in search of rescue. Like La Pérouse himself, the precise fate of these men has never been discovered.

The Mysterious Moai of Easter Island

In addition to being the most remote island on earth, Easter Island is known for its stone giants—the enormous sculptures called *moai,* which are carved from volcanic ash. La Pérouse was not the first or last to wonder how the Polynesians erected these mammoth statues.

Though the statues' origin is uncertain, historians believe the *moai* were sculpted sometime between the fifteenth and seventeenth centuries. The largest of the *moai* is over seventy-one feet tall and is estimated to weigh up to 165 tons. The smallest standing *moai* is just under four feet tall. In addition to the several hundred *moai* erected on the coastlines, archaeologists have found many more that were completed but never transported or raised. The *moai* may be depictions of Easter Island's chiefs and may also have been connected with the Polynesians' gods.

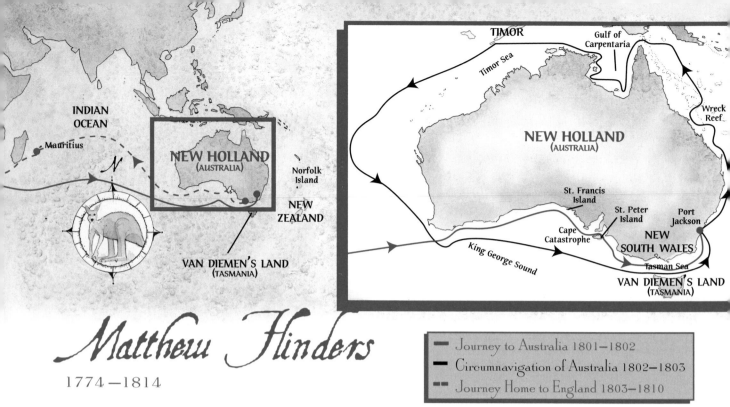

Matthew Flinders

1774—1814

— Journey to Australia 1801—1802
— Circumnavigation of Australia 1802—1803
-- Journey Home to England 1803—1810

Matthew Flinders, the man who would chart Australia's coastlines and give the continent its name, was born on March 16, 1774, in Lincolnshire, England. He attended school only until he was fifteen but continued to teach himself the sciences afterward. He became interested in the sea after reading Daniel Defoe's novel Robinson Crusoe and entered the navy just before turning sixteen.

In 1791, Flinders served with Captain Bligh on a trip to transport breadfruit trees from Tahiti to the West Indies. Bligh had achieved notoriety on his first journey to Tahiti, which had ended in a tragic mutiny. Bligh himself had sailed under the great Captain James Cook, and Flinders absorbed all he could on the expedition, particularly with regard to providing rations with the appropriate nutrition to avoid scurvy.

In 1794, Flinders served on the *Reliance,* which was transporting a new governor. John Hunter was to be Governor of New South Wales, an area of present-day Australia. This continent, then referred to as New Holland, was largely unexplored by Europeans. Only two English settlements were there: one on Norfolk Island and the other in Port Jackson, near present-day Sydney. Flinders also made

several important coastal explorations in a small cutter called the *Tom Thumb.* In the slightly larger sloop *Norfolk,* Flinders became the first to circumnavigate Van Diemen's Land, today called Tasmania.

With these accomplishments and a reputation as a meticulous navigator and chart maker, Flinders wrote a letter to Joseph Banks, the highly influential president of the Royal Geographical Society, suggesting an expedition to further explore New Holland. Impressed by Flinders, Banks agreed to organize and finance the journey. Flinders was given the ship *Investigator,* one hundred feet long but far from new. Flinders organized a crew of eighty-eight men, including a naturalist, a painter, a botanist, and a mining specialist. The focus of his expedition was just as strongly on science as on exploration.

Investigator sailed for New Holland on July 18, 1801, arriving at King George Sound on December 6. Proceeding east, Flinders and the crew would spend the next sixteen months making meticulous and highly detailed charts of the coastline, taking magnetic readings, and collecting plant specimens. Once past the islands of St. Peter and St. Francis, they were in unexplored waters. Their progress was excellent in spite of a tragic accident in February 1802. A cutter out rechecking some readings sank, and all eight hands aboard were drowned. Flinders named the place Cape Catastrophe.

In April, Flinders encountered his rival, French explorer Nicolas Baudin, on the ship *La Géographe*. Flinders had known the French were also exploring in the area, and the two commanders spoke for a while. Though the exchange was cordial, the French would later claim some of Flinders's discoveries as their own.

Investigator next stopped at the colony at Port Jackson. Flinders had now completely charted the southern coast of the continent, disproving the suspicion that a strait existed between New Holland and New South Wales. While in Port Jackson he established a very good friendship with the local governor, P. G. King. The friendship would be highly valuable to him later in the journey.

Flinders resumed circumnavigating the continent, but by November, *Investigator* was suffering from very serious leaks. The carpenter estimated that in good weather the ship could remain repairable and seaworthy for perhaps another six months. Low on rations, the men were also beginning to get scurvy, and four died. Flinders had no choice but to return to Port Jackson. There Governor King was able to provide Flinders with a small replacement ship named *Porpoise*.

On August 10, 1803, Flinders took *Porpoise* and two other ships and continued around the coast. Only one week later,

Matthew Flinders

Porpoise and one other ship, the *Cato*, were dashed onto a reef and wrecked. From the two ships, ninety-four men survived and took shelter on a sandbar. Flinders and the *Cato*'s captain took the surviving cutter and sailed back the seven hundred miles to Port Jackson to request that rescue ships be sent out for the marooned men waiting on what Flinders named Wreck Reef.

This time aboard the *Cumberland*, Flinders again headed around Australia's coast and picked up the stranded crew. The *Cumberland* was tiny, and only ten men were selected to accompany Flinders and his valuable charts back to England. The rest of the men would travel later, on a larger ship. But Flinders's bad luck continued. The *Cumberland* began to leak, and Flinders sought help at Port Louis on the island of Mauritius. The French governor of Mauritius interviewed Flinders. France and England were again at war, and the governor had already been told Flinders was suspected of searching for territory to establish British military bases in the area. Flinders was detained by the governor and would remain in custody for six long years.

He was finally released and returned to

England in 1810, his health and spirit deeply damaged. He spent the next three years working on his account of *Investigator*'s expedition, which he had been prevented from doing while in detention on Mauritius. By the time he finished the book, he was seriously ill. The work was titled *A Voyage to Terra Australis*. On June 26, 1814, he received word that the first published copy of the book had been presented to Joseph Banks. Several weeks later, Flinders was dead.

Though his bad luck prevented Flinders from receiving the credit and fame he was due during his lifetime, he is now considered second only to Captain Cook in his accomplishments in the Australian Pacific.

Captain Bligh and the Mutiny on the Bounty

When the Royal Geographical Society's Joseph Banks wanted to import breadfruit trees from Tahiti to the West Indies, naval officer William Bligh was appointed to carry out the plan. Bligh, having accompanied Captain Cook on his third voyage, was considered well qualified for the position. He and his forty-seven men sailed from England and arrived in Tahiti in October 1788.

For the next five months, Bligh's crew worked to transplant the breadfruit trees to pots on board. The men enjoyed the quiet paradise and the friendly locals of Tahiti. When Bligh discovered in February 1789 that the line to his main anchor had been cut, almost setting the ship adrift, he was not able to find out if it was a discontented Tahitian or one of his own crewmen who was responsible.

In April, Bligh determined they had all the plants that they required, and the *Bounty* set sail in the direction of the Tonga Islands. But his men weren't happy about leaving the island paradise. In the middle of the night, Bligh was forced at knifepoint into a small lifeboat, along with eighteen of his men who had refused to support the mutiny.

Captain Bligh was able to set a course for Tofua, part of the Tonga Island group, where he obtained more supplies. From there, he navigated the little boat 3,618 miles to Timor, an island northwest of Australia. At Timor, Bligh found himself and his men transport back to England.

The mutineers, unable to agree on much, ended up on various islands in the vicinity of Tahiti. Presuming Bligh was dead, they did not believe anyone would come searching for them. But the ship *Pandora* had been dispatched from England to arrest any mutineers who could be found. While some were captured and returned to England to face trial, others died in local skirmishes or remained successfully hidden.

Though Captain Bligh had a long and notable career in the navy, he is most famous for the incident of the mutiny on the *Bounty*.

This replica of the HMS *Bounty* was constructed for the 1962 film *Mutiny on the Bounty*.

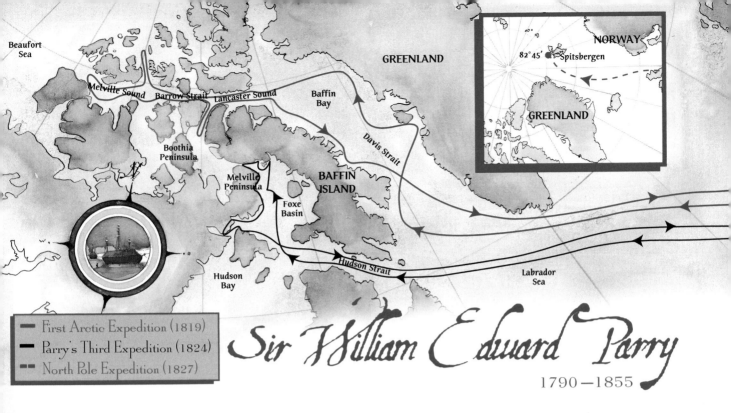

- First Arctic Expedition (1819)
- Parry's Third Expedition (1824)
- North Pole Expedition (1827)

Sir William Edward Parry

1790—1855

William Edward Parry was seemingly destined for the sea. Born in Bath, England, he joined the navy at only thirteen. It was a busy time in the final years of the British war with Napoleon and the War of 1812 against the United States. Parry's intelligence and ambition did not go unnoticed by the navy's admiralty. In 1818, the navy chose Parry, an amateur astronomer, to join John Ross's expedition in search of the Northwest Passage.

It was on this voyage that Parry and Ross had a now-famous disagreement. Their two ships had sailed into Lancaster Sound, off the north coast of Baffin Island. Parry correctly believed that they were in a strait, or sea passage, that provided a water route west. Ross insisted the area was a bay, enclosed by land, and he famously claimed to have glimpsed a mountain range in the distance blocking off any open water. Ross named this mysterious range the Croker Mountains. The mountains were ultimately proved not to exist. Ross was teased in England about his "Crokers" for much of his life. When the navy decided to send another group back to the Arctic, Parry, not Ross, was chosen to command.

The first Arctic expedition at Parry's command left England in 1819 and became known for being the first British group to plan an overwinter stay in the Arctic. Parry paid careful attention to the men's diet and placed great importance on morale, planning numerous activities to keep everyone occupied. The long months of winter darkness, when temperatures grew so cold that the mercury froze in the thermometer, were therefore tolerated relatively well by the men. It was during this expedition that Parry sailed up Lancaster Sound, through the Barrow Strait, and into present-day Melville Sound. In doing so, he proved Ross's Croker Mountain barrier was not real, and he penetrated farther west than any previous Arctic expedition. On his return to England, the navy hailed Parry as a success.

Parry made two more naval voyages in search of the Northwest Passage. Though he did not match the accomplishments of his

THE ARCTIC AND ANTARCTICA

Captain William Edward Parry

the *Fury*. On the heels of a gale, the *Fury* was dashed on the ice and swept onto a beach. The damage could not be repaired, and Parry had to take all of the men aboard his ship, the *Hecla*, before returning to England.

With three Arctic expeditions of his own under his belt, Parry next turned his focus to the North Pole. Though newly wed to Isabella Stanley, Parry was eager to have his chance to be the first to the pole. In 1827, the navy agreed to send him and gave Parry two small boats designed to convert into sleds. He brought the boats with him on board the *Hecla* until they reached the polar ice pack. Then Parry set off toward the pole, with each of the two boat-sleds manned by twelve of his crewmen. Unlike the Inuit sleds pulled by dogs, the men themselves pulled Parry's sleds. It was backbreaking work.

Parry wrongly believed that the route from his position to the pole would be mostly open sea, with small patches of pack ice to cross in between. But the ice was thicker and heavier than it had been in years, lying like huge scattered boulders in the sea. Alternating between lifting the boats into and out of the water, the group made small advances over ice and sea. The drift of the ice further complicated matters. The entire pack was drifting

1819 journey, both trips were beneficial. He observed the culture and customs of a local Inuit tribe on his trip in 1821, gaining valuable geographical knowledge from them in the process. The third expedition, from 1824 to 1825, may now be best known for the spectacular shipwreck of one of Parry's vessels,

Two Kinds of Poles

There are actually two South Poles and two North Poles. The poles that explorers such as Shackleton and Amundsen wanted to reach are the *geographic* poles of the earth. But some sixteen hundred miles from the geographic South Pole lies the south magnetic pole. This pole never stays in exactly the same place and is found not with a map but with a compass. The magnetic poles are the only two places on earth where the magnetic field is vertical. The force is downward at the north magnetic pole and upward at the south magnetic pole. We see evidence of the earth's magnetic field whenever we use a compass. The magnetism causes the needle to point to magnetic north. But when used at one of the earth's two magnetic poles, a compass will not work accurately.

south. For every mile Parry and his men were able to push north, the ice pulled them back half a mile in the wrong direction. Still, by the time Parry called a halt to the effort and turned his exhausted men around, they had traveled farther north than any expedition in history: latitude 82 degrees and 45 minutes north. Half a century would pass before Parry's record was challenged.

Though Parry never reached the North Pole, his expeditions were still hailed as triumphant. He was knighted in 1829. Eager to remain near home with his new wife, Parry continued his work for the navy in England. He never returned to the Arctic, but for many decades he remained the model Arctic explorer to whom British navy commanders would compare themselves.

The Northwest Passage

Since the time of Columbus, the greatest single objective of European explorers was to find the Northwest Passage. Pictured as the ultimate shortcut, a northwest passage would have allowed trading ships to travel from Europe to Asia at the very top of the world, uninterrupted by any landmass. The nation that discovered and controlled the Northwest Passage would gain enormous wealth and power from the trade advantage such a shortcut to the riches of the Orient would bring. But in time, the race became for the glory of the conquest itself. Portugal, Spain, America, France, and Britain, among others, tried time and time again to be the first to find and map the passage. Well into the nineteenth century, the race continued to intensify. The explorers who made their names in this iciest of quests—men such as William Parry, John Ross, John Franklin, Fridtjof Nansen, and Roald Amundsen—became national heroes of epic proportions.

The riddle of the Northwest Passage was finally solved in 1905 by one of the world's most famous and accomplished explorers, Roald Amundsen. Amundsen, who one day would become the first man to reach the South Pole, took a small fishing vessel called the *Gjoa* and, passing Baffin Island on the north side, threaded his way around a series of islands, passed to the south of Victoria Island and Banks Island, and continued to the Bering Strait.

Amundsen's discovery was made with a combination of skill, experience, and good luck, combined with favorable weather conditions. The great irony was that no one could dictate the current, the thickness of the ice, or the severity of the winter, and only a very small vessel such as Amundsen's could negotiate the straits. After hundreds of years, the Northwest Passage had been found, but the prize itself was useless.

Roald Amundsen's ship, the *Gjoa*

NORTH POLE

Norwegian Sea

Spitsbergen

Franz Josef Land

SWEDEN

NORWAY

Barents Sea

Kara Sea

RUSSIA

Lena River

— Route of the Fram
— Route over Ice with Sled and Kayak
-- Return on Jackson's Relief Vessel

Fridtjof Nansen
1861—1930

One of the most acclaimed explorers of his day, Fridtjof Nansen was born in Norway in 1861. He was a zoologist by profession but had his first taste of the Arctic when he joined a sealing expedition to Greenland. His experience on that trip, during which the ship spent three weeks frozen into the ice, shaped his future interest in and experiments with navigation through polar ice.

In 1881, news of the *Jeanette*'s expedition to the North Pole had traveled around the world. Frozen into the ice, the *Jeanette* had drifted for twenty-one months before finally being crushed. In the following years, items from the shipwreck were found almost three thousand miles away in southwest Greenland.

Nansen began to wonder if a ship could be designed to be *deliberately* frozen into the pack ice, using the pack's movement to travel just as a ship uses the wind and the currents to sail. A small ship with sloping sides and heavily reinforced ends theoretically could withstand the strength of the pack ice. The pressure would lift the ship up onto the ice, where it would travel safely. When the ice thawed, the ship should simply drop back into the sea.

Though many considered his theory

ridiculous, Nansen obtained support from the Norwegian government and began planning an expedition that would attempt to reach the North Pole. Like his ship, his team was small in size, numbering only twelve men. Nansen personally oversaw every aspect of the preparations, from the design of the ship to the size and makeup of the cooking equipment. His knowledge of skis, sleds, dogs, and kayaks allowed his team to be the most durable and versatile of its day. Nansen had been the first polar explorer to travel by skis, on his 1888 attempt to cross the polar ice cap. Now he designed special skis and sleds himself. His planning was so thorough that he even took lessons in the Inuit language. Nansen left nothing to chance.

The *Fram* sailed in June 1893 from Norway, crossed the icy hazards of the Kara

Sea, and proceeded along the Siberian coast as far as possible before reaching the ice pack. There was no going back. Nansen had packed enough supplies to last for more than three years. Close to the mouth of the Lena River, Nansen allowed the pack ice to surround the ship and freeze her in. As designed, the crushing ice simply lifted the ship out of harm's way, and the ship began to drift north. Maintaining the ship and carrying out periodic scientific observations helped to occupy the men during the long months of waiting that followed. They would continue to wait for two and a half years.

Eventually Nansen's reading of the course the *Fram* was taking showed him that the ship would not be swept directly over the North Pole. Ever ambitious, Nansen decided to take a sled and dog team directly onto the ice and attempt to reach the pole, then turn around and return to the *Fram*. The overland expedition would take three sleds and twenty-eight dogs, as well as Nansen's homemade snowshoes and several kayaks. Hjalmar Johansen would accompany him.

Nansen began the dash for the pole in March 1895. Although he reached farther north than any past explorer, the condition of the uneven, rough blocks of ice forced him to turn back. Regardless of whether they reached the pole, Nansen now knew they would never be able to find the *Fram* again. The plan was to head for Franz Josef Land to the south and spend the winter there. Nansen kept expecting to see it on the horizon, but it did not appear.

By now it was mid-June, the snow was turning to slush underfoot, and the pack ice in the sea was breaking apart. Nansen and Johansen had no choice but to transfer their supplies to the kayaks. They had already killed their dogs for food, and now the very ice beneath their feet was breaking up. Kayaking across open water, they would climb back onto ice, switch supplies over to

Fridtjof Nansen

the sled, and pull them along until they came to water again.

They traveled in this way day after day until July, when Nansen caught sight of an island in the distance. It was uninhabited, but Nansen and Johansen built themselves a shelter of stones and animal skins and began hunting for food. They remained on the island for almost ten months, then they began to travel south again, hoping to reach an island closer to Franz Josef Land.

It was now June 1896. While making breakfast at a makeshift camp, Nansen heard a dog barking. Following the sound, he was stunned to come across an Englishman walking toward him. The man was Frederick Jackson, who was leading his own expedition to the North Pole. The two Norwegians were fed by the astonished Jackson and his party, and as soon as they were able, they traveled back to Norway on Jackson's relief vessel. Shortly after arriving home, Nansen was ecstatic to receive the news that the *Fram* had just safely sailed into the harbor.

Nansen was widely hailed as a hero on his return. Though he had not reached the pole, his experiment with traveling in the pack ice was a success, and the resulting data proved that the area surrounding the North Pole is largely composed of ice and water, not land.

In his later years, Nansen became a devoted supporter of human rights, organizing refugee resettlement and establishing funds for Russian famine victims.

Dogsleds

The key to success that many Arctic explorers ignored was the simple method of adapting Inuit customs. The Inuit used sleds pulled by dogs, and no one was better qualified to know the best way to travel over the ice. British naval officers such as William Edward Parry and Robert Falcon Scott had a strong resistance to using dog power to supplement man power, believing man's efforts alone should be enough. Norwegians such as Nansen and Roald Amundsen and American Robert Peary had no

such reluctance. Peary even studied dogsled-handling techniques for two years. It is no coincidence that the first men to reach the North and the South Poles both relied on dogsleds.

Inuit sleds were made of wood and known as *komatiks*. The sleds could be loaded with supplies and pulled by teams of Alaskan or Canadian huskies bred to prosper in the bitter Arctic conditions. The pulling power of these animals more than made up for the extra supplies of dog food required. Polar travelers whose greatest priority was efficiency acknowledged that speed often required heartlessness—dogs that pulled sleds on the first leg of a journey might be eaten by the men on the way home.

A member of Roald Amundsen's expedition stands with his sled dogs.

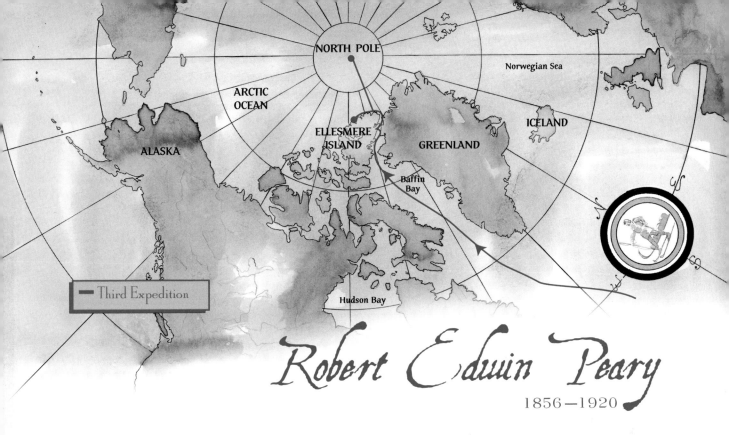

Robert Edwin Peary
1856–1920

Robert Peary possessed the greatest obsession to reach the North Pole of any explorer of his time. How far he was willing to go to secure fame is still a matter for argument.

Born in Pennsylvania in 1856, Peary developed his keen interest in the Arctic in childhood. He read every account written by the northern explorers that he could get his hands on. He began his career as an explorer with several expeditions to then largely unexplored Greenland. Even in his early expeditions, his character was evident—convinced others were plotting against him, he was extremely possessive of his right to explore without competition. Other members of his expedition were prohibited from writing or lecturing about the voyage and had to hand over their personal papers and diaries to Peary.

Like the legendary Norwegian explorer Roald Amundsen, Peary understood that the native Inuit could teach him valuable information about traveling in the Arctic. He adapted the Inuit fur clothing and boots, used dogsleds to haul supplies, and built snow houses for shelter instead of carrying tents.

Peary made three attempts to reach the North Pole, the last two in a specially designed ship called the *Roosevelt,* named for President Theodore Roosevelt. His longtime African American servant, Matthew Henson, accompanied Peary on all of his expeditions. Some historians have suggested that Peary felt comfortable having Henson and several Inuit accompany him on the dash for the pole because, as nonwhites, they would not receive equal credit for the accomplishment. Peary gave neither the Inuit nor Matthew Henson the praise they deserved. Henson, in particular, was a fully experienced explorer in his own right and had mastered the Inuit language so that he could interpret for Peary. But in Peary's eyes, Henson was only his servant.

Peary's third and final expedition in search of the North Pole sailed from the United States on July 6, 1908. Peary knew that he was lucky to get a third chance and that if he did not reach the North Pole this time, he would never get to try again. His

Peary stands on the main deck of the *Roosevelt*.

body of his party back, feeling his sole chance was to make a dash with only Henson, four Inuit, and several dog teams. It was during this week of supposedly traveling some 130 miles to the pole and back that Peary's account began to unravel. He later reported reaching the North Pole on April 7.

All explorers took sextant readings and observations to provide a daily record of their position. Though Peary usually shared these sextant readings with Matthew Henson, he did not on April 7. Peary's journal for that day, a day of which he had dreamed for decades, is recorded on a separate sheet of paper. No readings or observations appear in his regular journal during the time he spent at the pole itself.

In the years following Peary's return to New York, his claim on the pole was officially accepted, though rumors circulated questioning his report. Gradually his claims were investigated more thoroughly. It is now believed that based on Peary's position when he turned back his main party, he would have had to travel over forty miles a day to reach the pole when he claimed. This is more than four times as fast as any explorer has ever been able to travel in the Arctic, including

desperation to be the first was enormous. For years he had dreamed of winning fame by reaching the pole, and he had spared no effort or expense to make his dream come true. He must have been deeply disturbed, on reaching the Inuit community of Etah, to hear that fellow American Frederick Cook had apparently left in a run for the pole some three months earlier. Peary pressed on with all possible speed.

In his now-established routine, Peary sent Henson ahead with several Inuit to clear the trail, lay in food supplies, and build snow houses. Forced to halt their progress when areas of open water prevented them from crossing the ice, Peary grew increasingly pressed to hurry. He ultimately sent the main

Matthew Henson

one contemporary expedition on snow-mobiles. And though it is possible his sloppy record keeping is because he never expected to need proof of reaching the pole, it seems equally likely that he had no proof to give.

It is difficult to prove a negative, so it will probably never be known if Peary was the first man to reach the North Pole or if he deliberately created a false record. Whatever the case, Peary did achieve fame, and the mystery of his whereabouts on April 7, 1909, will never be forgotten.

The Truth About Frederick Cook

Peary may have benefited from the controversy surrounding his rival, Frederick Cook. On returning to the United States, Peary learned that Cook announced he had reached the pole himself in April 1908, a year before Peary. Cook had then become stranded and eventually made his way to the Greenland village of Anoatok with two Inuit companions. A more likable personality than Peary, Cook enjoyed popularity and instant fame when he returned claiming to have reached the pole. It was the custom of the time to give an explorer the benefit of the doubt. In the media storm of reporters and lectures following Cook's return, few openly questioned his claim. But one vocal accuser was Robert Peary himself, who believed Cook was lying. A war of words sprang up between the two, with rival New York newspapers taking sides. At first it seemed Cook had more support. But as time went by, Cook still did not produce any record of positional observations that any explorer would have kept in his log. If Peary's proof was missing crucial information, Cook's proof did not exist at all.

Claiming to have left all his documentation behind in the Arctic, Cook eventually produced a typewritten record of his journey that was widely believed to be false. He circulated far-fetched stories of a plot to steal his Arctic diaries from him. Public opinion began to turn. Now his earlier claim of being the first man to summit Mount McKinley also came under investigation. The once-whispered rumors that he had falsified the climbing claim were proved when experts studied a photograph of him on the summit and found the photograph was not authentic. Cook's fall from grace was swift. Almost by default, the realization that Cook had faked his account of reaching the pole made Peary's account ring more true. The possibility that both had faked their achievements seemed too outrageous to believe.

Frederick Cook, in his top hat, stands in front of a New York City crowd.

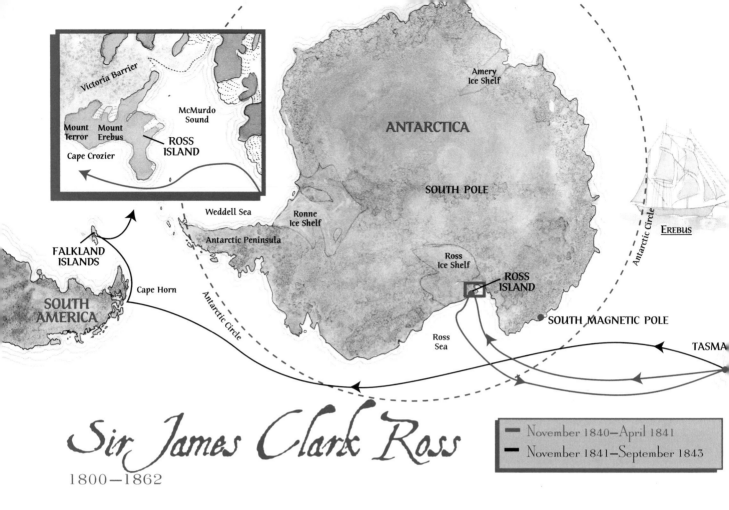

Sir James Clark Ross
1800–1862

— November 1840–April 1841
— November 1841–September 1843

By the time explorer James Ross turned his attention to Antarctica, he had already established a reputation as a successful and bold Arctic explorer. Born in London in 1800, Ross took to the sea early, joining the Royal Navy as a very young man. Serving aboard a ship under the command of his uncle, explorer John Ross, he went along on several early expeditions in search of the highly prized Northwest Passage. When explorer William Edward Parry led journeys to the north, attempting to find both the Northwest Passage and the North Pole, Ross again went along. Only in his twenties, James Clark Ross was already one of the most seasoned Arctic travelers in England.

When Ross accepted the second-in-command position of his uncle's 1829 quest for the Northwest Passage, he had no idea he and the crew would be marooned in the area of the Boothia Peninsula for four winters. Frozen into the harbor and stranded, the energetic and curious Ross took advantage of the opportunity to explore the Boothia coastline by dogsled. During his frequent trips, he mapped over four hundred miles of previously un-known territory. On one of these journeys, he achieved his greatest accomplishment to date: he located the north magnetic pole, making a permanent name for himself as an accomplished Arctic explorer and scientist.

In 1839, the British Royal Navy was ready to send an expedition south to explore the Antarctic. Two goals of the expedition were to make magnetic experiments and observations and to locate the south magnetic pole. Few men if any were more qualified to head such an expedition than James Clark Ross. The Royal Navy gave Ross two ships, the *Erebus* and the *Terror,* which was captained by Ross's friend Commander Francis Crozier. Ross knew that a successful expedition required a crew that was well fed and comfortable, and he outfitted his two ships accordingly.

The *Erebus* and the *Terror* departed England in October 1839. Their first task was to sail south to Tasmania and build a permanent structure for scientific research. Ross spent the next four years making exploratory voyages in the Antarctic Circle.

While in Tasmania, Ross spent time with Governor John Franklin, another renowned Arctic explorer. From Franklin, Ross learned the latest news concerning French and American efforts to locate the south magnetic pole. They had just explored the territory in which Ross had intended to begin. Rather than follow the route already established by other nations, Ross decided to change his destination. He would head for a more easterly coast of Antarctica that had yet to be explored.

Having completed their scientific work, the two ships left Tasmania in November of 1840. On New Year's Day of 1841, they sailed across the Antarctic Circle, carefully negotiating their way through the pack ice. One of Ross's first discoveries was that a mass of land lay between their position and the south magnetic pole. This obstacle would prevent them from being the first to locate the magnetic pole. But the series of discoveries that lay ahead would more than make up for the disappointment.

A quick glance at a map will attest to the immensity of their findings: a large number of areas were named by or for the Ross expedition. They came through the present-day McMurdo Sound, beyond which they discovered the awe-inspiring barrier of the Ross Ice Shelf. Its ice cliffs towered two hundred feet over the ocean, and its interior was the size of a small country. The map shows the Ross Ice Shelf facing Ross Island and the Ross Sea, near Cape Crozier, Mount Erebus, and Mount Terror. When reported back in Tasmania, this series of discoveries won Ross's expedition the reputation as the most important Antarctic journey of its time.

Leaving Tasmania again in November 1841, Ross continued his exploration and charting. Then, at long last, the ships made their way home, arriving in England in September 1843. Almost immediately, the navy wished to refit the *Erebus* and *Terror* and send Ross back to the Arctic Circle for another attempt to locate the Northwest Passage. But Ross was happy to be home after over four years in the southern seas, and he turned down the command. Ross's friend John Franklin took the job instead. The disappearance of Franklin, his ship, and his crew became one of the most widely talked-about mysteries of the nineteenth century. Ross himself would command one of the search parties dispatched to locate Franklin and his men, but they were never found. Well aware that he had come very close to commanding the ships that had disappeared so mysteriously, Ross contented himself with spending his final years quietly and firmly on land.

Artifacts from the Franklin expedition

The Lost Franklin Expedition

Though Sir John Franklin's accomplishments of Arctic exploration are not unusually significant, his disappearance resulted in one of the greatest mysteries of the British Victorian era. Like explorers for three centuries before him, Sir John Franklin undertook an expedition to find the Northwest Passage. At fifty-nine, he was considered old to head up such a journey, but he was in good health and known to be a capable and experienced commander. His expedition set out in May 1845, on the ships *Erebus* and *Terror*, which Sir James Clark Ross had taken to Antarctica five years earlier.

In 1848, with no word from or about Franklin, worry began to spread in England. A rescue expedition was sent after him. Over the next eleven years, more than forty expeditions went to the Arctic in search of Franklin and his lost men. Even after it was widely accepted that there could be no survivors, search parties continued looking. Some hoped to provide an explanation of what had happened to the 129 men, and some hoped to collect a cash reward.

The lure of the Franklin mystery became almost as great as the lure of the Northwest Passage itself. With each passing year, the public's appetite grew larger for some resolution to the riddle of the lost men. The British navy's interest and commitment began to wane, but they did not count on the tireless determination of Franklin's wife, Lady Jane Franklin. For years following the disappearance, she spared neither effort nor cost to encourage and fund private expeditions to keep looking for him.

In 1854, searcher John Rae returned to England claiming that Inuit on the Boothia Peninsula had seen forty starving white men several years earlier. Rae brought back several relics purchased from the Inuit, including a medal belonging to Franklin. The fact that he also claimed that some of the starving men had cannibalized their dead mates fits with modern archaeological evidence. But Lady Franklin was reluctant to accept the story as the end of the search.

It was not until 1859 that anyone could form a significant theory of what had happened. In that year, explorer Francis Leopold McClintock sailed in search of Franklin, following clues collected over the last decade. Inuit near northern Boothia Peninsula sold more relics from the Franklin expedition to the searchers and this time detailed where two great ships, obviously the *Erebus* and the *Terror*, had been crushed and swallowed by the ice. McClintock himself began to come across relics and finally found a skeleton in a navy uniform. With the body were papers identifying the man as part of the *Terror*'s crew. Finally he found a heap of stones called a cairn. In the cairn was a note detailing some of the expedition's last months. It stated that the men abandoned the ships after becoming stuck in the ice. A number of men, including Franklin, had since died, and the survivors were walking south toward Back's Fish River. It is now clear the men died one after the other on the walk south, weakened by scurvy, starvation, and lead poisoning from canned food.

The last discovery was a wooden lifeboat on a sled, containing over a thousand pounds of additional supplies, including silverware. Two skeletons were also inside. Why the men would have dragged such heavy articles with them is still a matter of debate. Modern evidence from examination of some of the expedition's remains showed lethal levels of lead, which may have caused the men to suffer mental disturbances. But this is only one explanation for their bizarre behavior.

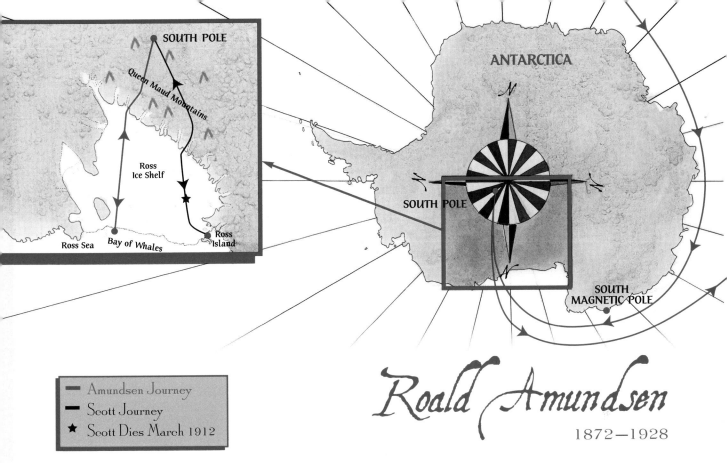

SOUTH POLE

Queen Maud Mountains

Ross
Ice Shelf

Ross Sea   Bay of Whales   Ross Island

ANTARCTICA

N

SOUTH POLE

N

N

N

SOUTH MAGNETIC POLE

— Amundsen Journey
— Scott Journey
★ Scott Dies March 1912

Roald Amundsen
1872–1928

Roald Amundsen first became acquainted with the dangers and thrills of polar exploration as a teenager, when he read John Franklin's account of a brutal trip to the Arctic. Raised in the cold and rugged country of Norway, Amundsen was a natural outdoorsman with great endurance and a natural ability on skis. When he was still a teenager, he made his first polar expedition, accompanying the Belgian group that became the first to winter in the Antarctic.

*I*n 1903, Amundsen obtained his own small vessel. Two years later, he successfully navigated the Northwest Passage through to the Bering Strait. In succeeding where so many explorers had failed, Amundsen became a legend. Like many of his peers, Amundsen longed to be the first to the North Pole. On the heels of his success completing the Northwest Passage, Amundsen convinced world-famous Norwegian explorer Fridtjof Nansen to lend Amundsen his ship, the *Fram*. Nansen also provided him with a wealth of information on how to travel safely and quickly in the challenging polar conditions.

At some time during his preparations to reach the North Pole, Amundsen heard someone else had already reached it. It was often years after such a trip before explorers could get back to civilization, and now two claims were voiced. Frederick Cook announced he had arrived at the pole on April 21, 1908, and Robert Peary claimed to have reached the pole the following year. Amundsen began to consider changing his goal from the North to the South Pole. When he heard that British naval officer Robert Falcon Scott would be leading a team to the Antarctic pole, Amundsen's mind was made up. He would make his own try for the South Pole, but his goal would remain completely secret. Attempts to reach the pole were extremely competitive, and if Scott were to learn of Amundsen's intentions too soon, the British might leave early and gain a large advantage. It was not until the *Fram* was fully provisioned and sailing south that Amundsen sent Scott a cable about his new plan. By then it was too late for anyone to protest.

Amundsen arrived at the Bay of Whales in the Ross Sea in January 1911. He intended to build his base camp here, across the bay from Ross Island, where Scott and the British party would be wintering. Amundsen planned to build a hut in which he and his eight men would spend the winter. As soon as the weather permitted in the spring, they would make their dash to the South Pole. The *Fram* departed after the winter camp was completed, and Amundsen and his men were on their own.

It was not an idle winter. Each man had a full morning and afternoon of work assigned, adding finishing touches to the hut, packing provisions, and strengthening the dogsleds that would carry their supplies. Amundsen was extremely detail-oriented and highly efficient in his planning. These characteristics would give his team a crucial edge over the British. His men were all experienced skiers and well trained in working alongside sled dogs, which would allow them to travel with great speed over the snow and ice. Amundsen prepared his men for every possible situation, enforcing an exercise regimen and nutritious diet to develop strength and endurance. A key aspect of his plan, efficient if also heartless, was that their dogs would pull the sleds south, then be killed and eaten when the supplies were used and the sleds lightened.

Amundsen sent men ahead to lay in a series of supplies in snow cairns that would also serve as direction markers. In October 1911, all of Amundsen's extensive preparations had been completed. With four men, four sleds, and fifty-two dogs, Amundsen set out in the direction of the pole. In the beginning, the snow was hard and flat. The dogs pulled the sleds while the men skied alongside, and they were able to progress as much as twenty miles a day. Several weeks into the journey, the snow became more hilly and uneven, and they could clearly see a mountain range in the distance. The ascent of the Queen Maud

Icebergs

Approximately 90 percent of the world's ice is found on or around Antarctica. When enormous chunks of glaciers or ice shelves break off and drop into the sea, they form icebergs. The bergs can reach massive proportions, rising hundreds of feet out of the sea and extending four times that distance downward. A ship colliding with such a berg can be torn open and sunk, as evidenced by the most famous of ice disasters—the sinking of the ocean liner *Titanic*. Bergs the size of city buildings may float in the sea for years before eventually melting. Occasionally bergs of gigantic proportions form. One glimpsed by satellite in 1987 measured eighty miles from end to end!

Iceberg in Antarctica

Mountains would prove to be the most challenging obstacle they would face. At the top, half the dogs were shot and used for food. The climb took more than four days, and now the weather turned against them. For ten days, they faced one snowstorm after another. But Amundsen's planning had paid off, and the men were physically up to the challenge.

By December 8, they had less than one hundred miles to go. The weather cleared, and Amundsen knew he was nearing his goal. What he could not know was how Scott's party had fared and whether the British had beaten them to the pole. Amundsen would not have to remain in suspense much longer. On December 14, 1911, Amundsen and his party reached the South Pole. It was pristine. Amundsen was indeed the winner, and he planted the Norwegian flag on the spot as a proclamation to all who followed that the Norwegians had been there first.

Amundsen's triumphs in the Northwest

Roald Amundsen

Passage and the South Pole made him world-famous. He never lost his love of polar travel and, in his later years, undertook several voyages by airplane and airship over the North Pole. In 1928, he took a small plane north to search for a missing polar explorer and died when his plane went down.

The Tragedy of Robert Falcon Scott

The competition between Roald Amundsen and Robert Falcon Scott to reach the South Pole was polite but deadly serious. The two men had little in common. Scott was a British naval officer who placed great emphasis on discipline, duty, and rank. Scott possessed a burning ambition to reach the pole, but he lacked the organizational abilities and experience needed to survive such a demanding and dangerous journey. He and his men set out from their camp on Ross Island, dividing the pulling of supply sleds between men, ponies, and dogs and supported by two motor sleds. The motor sleds and ponies proved useless, and soon Scott's men were growing exhausted and frostbitten under the burden of the extra labor in the bitter cold.

When the party finally reached the pole on January 16, they received a deadly blow to their spirits. The Norwegian flag was flying, and a note Amundsen left at the site confirmed that Scott and his men had lost the race to the pole. Weakened and disheartened, they began to make the return journey to base camp, but exhaustion and bitter weather overtook them. Taking shelter in a tent during a blizzard, Scott and his men died, leaving behind a farewell letter that read, "These rough notes and our dead bodies must tell the tale. . . ."

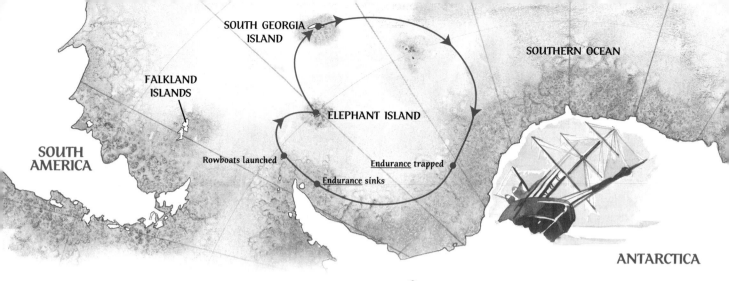

Sir Ernest Shackleton

1874–1922

When the rescue vessel carrying Ernest Shackleton and his twenty-seven-man crew arrived in Chile, it was as if they were returning from the dead. Shackleton and the crew of <u>Endurance</u> had been given up as lost many months earlier, when they disappeared during the British Imperial Trans-Antarctic Expedition. Already one of the world's best-known Antarctic explorers, Shackleton would become a living legend when the story of his doomed expedition and heroic rescue reached the world.

Born in Ireland in 1874, Shackleton was one of ten children in a crowded yet comfortable home. His father was a physician whose income was sufficient not only to provide for but also to educate all of his children. But Shackleton was no great lover of school. He preferred instead to read books and magazines, which sparked his imagination.

Shackleton had his first taste of adventure at sixteen, when he left home to work on the trading ships of the mercantile marine. When he heard of an upcoming expedition that would attempt to reach the South Pole, Shackleton joined up. The 1901 expedition, headed by Robert Falcon Scott, failed to reach the pole. But Shackleton's passion for Antarctica had been born. Even when Scott died on his next attempt to reach the pole in 1912, Shackleton was undaunted.

When Shackleton's British Imperial Trans-Antarctic Expedition got under way in 1914, the explorer had already achieved several important firsts on the continent. In 1908, he had come within one hundred miles of the South Pole, setting a new record. On that same expedition his men climbed to the summit of Mount Erebus. When he returned home to England, Shackleton was knighted by the queen.

Though the Norwegian Roald Amundsen became the first to reach the South Pole in 1911, no one had ever crossed Antarctica from one coast to the other. Much of the interior had never been seen or mapped. Shackleton intended to change that. It would be a trek of over eighteen hundred miles—something like walking from Maine to Florida, but in bitter and dangerous weather conditions.

Shackleton's ship was a three-masted sailing vessel called *Endurance*. She was made of oak, carried a coal-burning engine, and measured 144 feet long. On December 5, 1914, *Endurance* sailed for Antarctica from the last landfall on South Georgia Island. She would never reach her destination. The polar ice pack, always a danger to ships, was quite thick. It became more and more difficult to find a clear path through the water. By mid-January the ship could not move at all. *Endurance* and her crew were frozen into the pack ice. Their radio could not send a signal far enough to reach civilization, so there was no way to call for help.

Shackleton had no choice but to wait, hoping that the temperature would rise enough for some of the ice to break up. But the opposite happened. The ice gradually grew tighter and tighter. After eight months of waiting, the pressure of the ice ripped through *Endurance*'s wooden hull, and she began to sink. Shackleton ordered his men onto the ice with their sled dogs, some essential belongings, and *Endurance*'s three wooden lifeboats. For the next six months they camped out on the pack ice, supplementing their provisions with seal and penguin meat. Eventually the dogs, much loved by many of the crew, had to be eaten, too. When the ice finally began to break up beneath the camp, the men put their lifeboats into the water and rowed.

They landed on a small mountain of ice and rocks called Elephant Island. The island provided practically no shelter from the bitter Antarctic weather. Shackleton knew no one would come looking for them. He would have to seek help himself. Rigging one of the lifeboats with a sail, Shackleton set out with five of his men on a dangerous journey through the Southern Ocean. His goal was to get back to South Georgia Island, the only outpost of civilization between their position and Africa. South Georgia lay over eight hun-

Deckside portrait of Sir Ernest and Lady Emily Shackleton

dred miles away, beyond some of the most violent seas in the world. If they missed the tiny island, they would never survive in their open boat.

After two weeks sailing through violent typhoons and navigating with only a handheld sextant and a soggy map, Shackleton and his men reached the uninhabited side of South Georgia Island. Their safe arrival is considered one of the great accomplishments of navigation. With no time to lose, Shackleton and two of his men set out to climb the massive mountain range lying between their landing and a whaling station on the eastern coast. When they descended and staggered into the whaling station, the men were filthy, with long, matted beards and hair. They had trouble convincing people of their identities, since Shackleton and his men had long since

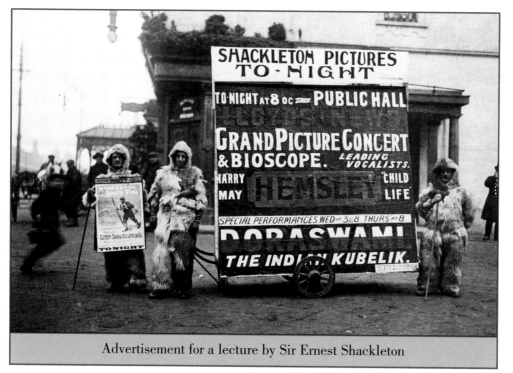
Advertisement for a lecture by Sir Ernest Shackleton

Shackleton was a shrewd and effective leader who inspired great loyalty not only in his men but also in his wife and children, who patiently endured his absences. In spite of all that had happened on *Endurance*, Shackleton organized yet another Antarctic expedition to the continent in 1922. His wife supported the plan, and a number of his *Endurance* crew eagerly volunteered to go with him again. But once again, the hand of fate intervened.

been given up for dead. But he soon convinced one of the whalers to sail with him back to Elephant Island to rescue his remaining twenty-two men.

The heavy pack ice forced the rescue ship to turn back, and it was not until his fourth attempt, in a Chilean boat called the *Yelcho*, that Shackleton was able to reach Elephant Island. It had been four months since he had left his men on the desolate island, and Shackleton feared many of them would be dead. As he approached the rocky beach, he could see men waving and shouting. Shackleton counted them through his binoculars. They were all there!

Sir Ernest Shackleton never accomplished the goals he set for his Antarctic expeditions. He never reached the pole, and he never crossed the continent. But he achieved immortality through the extraordinary leadership he displayed in bringing all twenty-seven of his men safely home after being stranded for almost two years.

As his ship lay anchored in the harbor of South Georgia Island, forty-seven-year-old Shackleton suffered a massive heart attack. He died as he had lived: restless, ambitious, and headed for the ice.

Penguins at the Antarctic

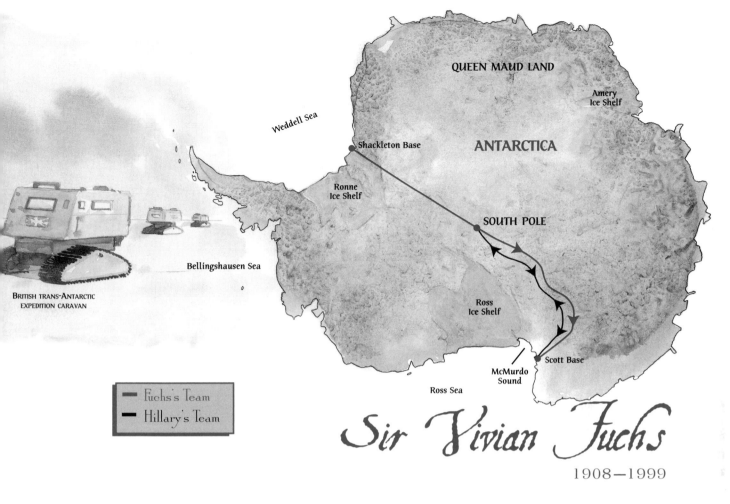

QUEEN MAUD LAND

Amery
Ice Shelf

Weddell Sea

Shackleton Base

ANTARCTICA

Ronne
Ice Shelf

SOUTH POLE

Bellingshausen Sea

Ross
Ice Shelf

BRITISH TRANS-ANTARCTIC
EXPEDITION CARAVAN

Scott Base

McMurdo
Sound

Ross Sea

— Fuchs's Team
— Hillary's Team

Sir Vivian Fuchs
1908—1999

When Vivian Fuchs felt the lure of Antarctica, the continent held some of the last heroic challenges for explorers. The nineteenth century was full of attempts to win glory in Antarctica, and as late as the 1950s, one prize was still up for grabs—the crossing of the continent from one coast to the other.

Vivian Fuchs was born in England in 1908 to a German father and an English mother. He first became interested in polar exploration when studying with his tutor, Sir James Wordie, a member of Shackleton's legendary 1914 Antarctica expedition. Fuchs studied to become a geologist and later accompanied Wordie on a 1929 expedition to east Greenland.

Fuchs served in Germany and Africa during World War II. At its close, he was appointed leader of a group that would eventually be called the British Antarctic Survey. For some years, Fuchs had secretly nursed the idea of revisiting Shackleton's trans-Antarctic expedition. In the years following the war, the nature of exploration in Antarctica had changed. The United States, England, Chile, and Argentina had all established bases and claimed land on the continent. The atmosphere became more cooperative. The world's first joint expedition, the Norwegian-British-Swedish Antarctic Expedition, took place from 1949 to 1952. The International Council of Scientific Unions began to plan a year of scientific research in which a number of countries could participate. It seemed the perfect time for Fuchs to realize his dream. With the backing of Sir James Wordie, Fuchs obtained the cooperation and financial support of New Zealand, South Africa, and Australia.

Like Shackleton, Fuchs divided his men

into two teams. Fuchs himself headed up the first team. Its advance party would create a winter base in the Weddell Sea area. After the hut and supplies were prepared, the main party would make the actual crossing of the continent. The second team would wait across Antarctica in the Ross Sea area, laying depots of supplies and establishing a route through to the final base. Edmund Hillary, a New Zealander known for his mountain-climbing abilities, headed the Ross Sea party.

Unlike Shackleton, Fuchs could take advantage of modern technology. The expedition's equipment included two seaplanes to scout ice conditions for the boats, four Sno-Cats (a tractorlike vehicle specially designed to drive over ice and snow), and a number of smaller tractors.

Fuchs's advance party sailed for the Weddell Sea in November 1955, facing a difficult and hazardous passage through the pack ice and losing some of their supplies in a storm. Fuchs and his main party arrived at the newly named Shackleton Base in November 1956. They would spend the winter on the base doing preparatory work. Fuchs and the rest of the team arrived at the Weddell base in February 1957.

By this time the advance party had finished unloading and preparing all of the supplies for the crossing. They did a remarkable job, in spite of the accident in the storm that caused much of their coal and timber and one of their small Ferguson tractors to be swept into the ocean. Across the continent, the Ross team had completed its base at McMurdo Sound, called the Scott Base. Using airplanes, they determined where best to lay the depots of supplies Fuchs's main party would use while making the crossing.

Fuchs was not ready to begin the crossing until November 24, 1957, about ten days behind schedule. He had to allow time for the seismic shots and gravity readings that would be taken every thirty and fifteen miles,

Vivian Fuchs after reaching the South Pole

respectively. Now that they knew the location of many of the crevasses, Fuchs hoped to make good time on the first leg of their journey. But only several days from base camp, a snow bridge collapsed under one of the Sno-Cats, leaving the vehicle suspended precariously with Fuchs and another man inside the cabin. They managed to crawl to safety, and the other tractors towed out the Sno-Cat.

Depending on conditions, they progressed between twenty and forty miles a day. On reaching the South Ice Station, where scientific observations were being carried out, there was a tense exchange of messages radioed between Fuchs and Hillary. Hillary, waiting on the Ross Sea side, had finished laying his depots ahead of schedule and gone ahead to the pole without authorization. He felt Fuchs had fallen so far behind schedule, he should consider stopping at the American South Pole Station and wintering there, continuing the second half of the journey the following year. Fuchs's response was firm—they would continue as scheduled.

Fuchs's party reached the South Pole on January 19, 1958, receiving great fanfare from the scientists and reporters there. They pressed on as soon as possible. They had come nine hundred miles in two months, but another 1,250 miles still lay ahead. Conditions were difficult, but no major catastrophes slowed them. They carefully descended the massive ice block called the Skelton Glacier. Now only about 130 miles lay between them and the Scott Base. On March 1, they had a record run—seventy-five miles in a single day. They were almost there.

On March 2, the Sno-Cats decked out in flags, Fuchs and his party arrived at the Scott Base. They had crossed the continent, traveling 2,158 miles in ninety-nine days. Fuchs's crossing was truly a miracle of the modern age.

Fuchs returned triumphant to England, where he was knighted and awarded a rare Special Gold Medal by the Royal Geographical Society. In his later years, he was director of the British Antarctic Survey and then president of the Royal Geographical Society. He died in England in 1999.

Sir Edmund Hillary

On the 1957–1958 expedition crossing Antarctica, Sir Vivian Fuchs was the star. But Edmund Hillary had already achieved fame by becoming the first person to reach the summit of Mount Everest in 1953.

The expedition began at a base camp 170 miles from Kathmandu in Nepal. After several weeks getting their bodies used to the high altitude and thin air, they began sending up teams to establish the upper camps on the mountain. Finally they were ready to make an attempt on the summit. Two teams would make the attempt: first Tom Bourdillon and Charles Evans, followed by Edmund Hillary and the local Sherpa climber Tenzing Norgay.

Sir Edmund Hillary and Tenzing Norgay after their ascent of Everest

The first team failed to reach the summit, and Hillary and Norgay had to wait several days for good weather. As soon as they could, they pushed upward. Two other team members and a Sherpa climbed ahead to lay out the route. Hillary and Norgay followed, carrying heavy loads. At almost twenty-eight thousand feet, the two groups met and shook hands. Hillary and Norgay prepared to press on to the summit, while the other three descended and rested.

Hillary and Norgay slept several hours in the tiny Camp IX, the highest camp ever set on the mountain at the time. Before dawn, they were climbing again, cutting steps of ice up the mountain face. The temperature was minus 27 degrees Celsius. After several hours of backbreaking labor, the South Summit was in sight. No one had ever climbed past the summit, but Hillary and Norgay felt strong enough. The final summit ridge was visible ahead. But it took them an hour to painstakingly negotiate a forty-foot crack in the ice on the final rock step leading to the top, a section of Everest now called the Hillary Step. Exhausted after climbing it, they proceeded carefully, cutting one step after another into the ice with their axes. Suddenly there was nowhere else to go. Edmund Hillary and Tenzing Norgay had become the first people in history to reach the summit of Mount Everest.

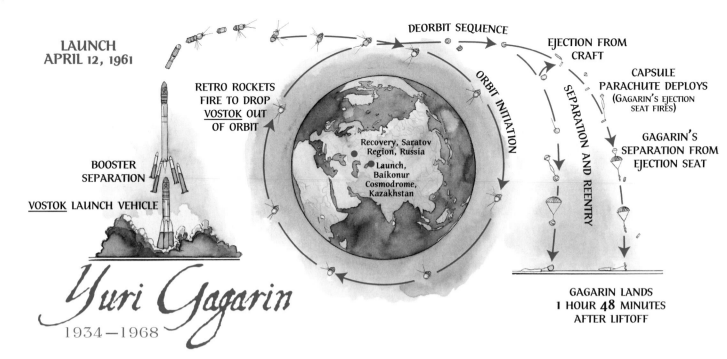

LAUNCH
APRIL 12, 1961

RETRO ROCKETS
FIRE TO DROP
VOSTOK OUT
OF ORBIT

BOOSTER
SEPARATION

VOSTOK LAUNCH VEHICLE

DEORBIT SEQUENCE

EJECTION FROM
CRAFT

CAPSULE
PARACHUTE DEPLOYS
(GAGARIN'S EJECTION
SEAT FIRES)

GAGARIN'S
SEPARATION FROM
EJECTION SEAT

ORBIT INITIATION

SEPARATION AND REENTRY

Recovery, Saratov
Region, Russia

Launch,
Baikonur
Cosmodrome,
Kazakhstan

GAGARIN LANDS
1 HOUR 48 MINUTES
AFTER LIFTOFF

Yuri Gagarin
1934—1968

For thousands of years people had looked to the stars with dreams and imagination. When Yuri Gagarin was born in a small Russian village in 1934, people were little closer to reaching space than they had been a century earlier. On the collective farm where he and his family worked, Gagarin's prospects were limited. However, his was a peaceful existence until 1941, when World War II arrived in Gagarin's front yard.

By 1942, hostile German soldiers had occupied the Gagarins' village near Gzhatsk. The soldiers killed many people and evicted the Gagarins from their home. The following spring, Yuri Gagarin and his sister were sent to a Nazi prison camp in Poland, where they were forced to do manual labor. Though their family had given them up for dead, the two children survived and returned home in 1945 after the Germans had withdrawn. Gagarin's character had now been established—he was coolheaded, strong, and a born survivor. These were characteristics that would serve him well as a pilot and would be partly responsible for his selection to train in the cosmonaut program.

At the age of sixteen, Gagarin apprenticed to learn the steel foundry trade and was accepted for a position at the city of Saratov's technical school. In Saratov, Gagarin saw signs advertising the local flying club. He spent every free hour at the club taking lessons. By the time he graduated from the technical school, he had acquired the skills to enter pilot school as a military cadet. Two years later, Yuri Gagarin was a Soviet air force pilot.

During his time at the Soviet Air Force Academy at Orenburg, Gagarin met and married Valentina Goryacheva, a medical technician. When Gagarin received his first posting at the isolated and bitterly cold Nikel air base, his wife went with him. It was there that their first child was born. It was not a pleasant place to live or work, but the young family settled in as best they could.

When a group of officials arrived on the air base looking for candidates for a new but unspecified program, Gagarin stood out. He had an excellent record from pilot school, and he was extremely physically fit. Though the nature of the new program remained unspoken, Gagarin and other pilots must have known there was a good possibility it was a space program. Just two years earlier, the Soviets had launched the first man-made satellites, *Sputnik 1* and *Sputnik 2*.

Rocket technology had developed rapidly during World War II. But it was not until the Soviets had their first major triumph in space with *Sputnik* that America seriously entered the space race. The next great prize in the race would be to get a man to outer space and back again. The mysterious teams were looking for candidates for just such a program. After many months looking at over two thousand candidates for their first space mission, the team had narrowed the list down to six. Gagarin was one of them.

The next phase for the chosen six, now called cosmonauts, was a series of tests to determine how they would react to the rigors of space travel. Training at a secret base called Star City, Gagarin was placed in an isolation chamber with changing levels of air pressure. He was spun around on a machine to approximate his physical response to the gravitational force he would encounter flying into space. He was plunged down an elevator shaft to achieve three seconds of gravity-free weightlessness. Though he did not enjoy many of the tests, Gagarin endured them all without complaint. Doctors were convinced that this cosmonaut had a good chance of going to outer space and back without suffering permanent physical damage.

Less than a week before the manned mission was scheduled to depart, Gagarin learned that he had been selected to be the first man to travel to outer space. On April 12, 1961, he was helped into his flight suit and transported to the launch area, where *Vostok 1* would carry him beyond the stratosphere. Gagarin was calm and collected in spite of the risks. Several unmanned test missions had not survived reentry to the earth's atmosphere, and scientists still did not know for certain the

1961 newspaper articles about Yuri Gagarin

effect the gravity-free environment would have on the human body. Any number of things might go wrong. But Gagarin remained cheerful as he climbed into the tiny capsule attached to the huge rocket.

Vostok 1 was launched at 9:07 a.m. As the rocket began to ascend, Gagarin radioed in frequent updates of his condition, stressing that he felt fine. Approximately three minutes after launch, the side-slung boosters detached as intended and fell away from Gagarin's capsule. He could now see through the portholes, noting the intense dark blue of the stratospheric level of the atmosphere. A mere nine minutes after launch, Gagarin had entered the earth's orbit. Now he experienced the state of weightlessness the scientists had worried about so much. It seemed to have little negative effect on the cosmonaut, and he radioed that the sensation was not at all unpleasant.

By 9:30 a.m., the final capsule-rocket separation had been successfully completed, and *Vostok 1* was headed east around the globe. *Vostok 1* flew over Siberia toward the Pacific, over America and the South Atlantic Ocean, and finally over West Africa and back over the Soviet Union, where the residents of a small village named Smelovka were about to get a surprise. Unlike future American spaceflights, the Soviet mission was not designed for a water splashdown. Gagarin's seat in the capsule was equipped with an ejection system, a propulsion pack, and a large parachute. As the capsule began to descend, Gagarin ejected. He then opened his parachute and floated down into a field, where he was soon surrounded by a group of stunned but curious farmers. In a mission that had lasted just 108 minutes, Gagarin and the Soviet Union had won the first critical prize in the space race.

Yuri Gagarin never again visited outer space. He continued working with Russia's space program, but the pressures of being a world celebrity took their toll on his personal life. When it was clear that he would never be allowed to take part in another space mission, he decided to return to his first love, flying planes. On what should have been a routine test flight with a fellow pilot in 1968, Gagarin's plane crashed in conditions of poor weather and limited visibility. Gagarin and his companion were killed. The precise cause of the crash was never determined.

Yuri Gagarin was the first person in history to enter outer space and view our world as a sphere from that perspective. His accomplishment inspired civilians and scientists alike and raised the bar for what could be accomplished in the realm of space.

Valentina Tereshkova

Just two years after the Soviet Union successfully sent the first man to outer space, they set their sights on sending the first woman. A loom operator at a mill and an expert parachuter in her spare time, Valentina Tereshkova was one of four candidates picked for the opportunity to fly a *Vostok* mission. The mission, *Vostok 6,* was to take place at the same time as *Vostok 5,* which would be piloted by a male cosmonaut, Valeri Bykovsky. Like all aspects of the Russian space program, Tereshkova's mission was top-secret. Even members of her family did not know she was going into space until they heard the live radio broadcast of the event.

Tereshkova trained for eighteen months before *Vostok 6* launched. She orbited the earth forty-eight times before reentry, after which she successfully ejected from her capsule and parachuted back to earth. She was awarded the Order of Lenin and the Hero of the Soviet Union Gold Star Medal and became a model to the world of the strength and potential of Soviet women.

Three women cosmonauts at Tyuratam, Kazakhstan, prior to the launch of *Vostok 6* on June 16, 1963. Left to right: Valentina Ponomareva, Irina Solovyeva, and Valentina Tereshkova.

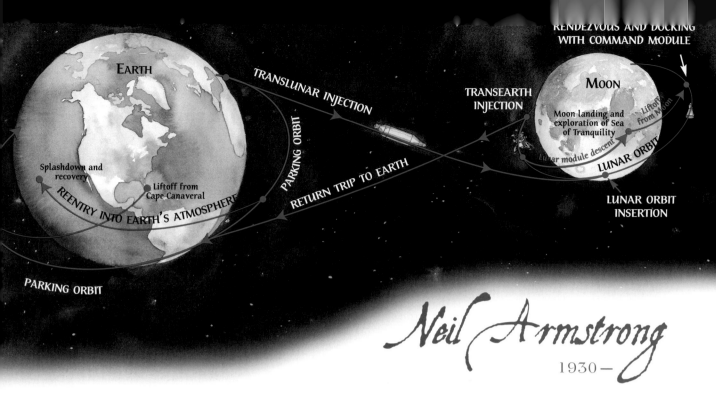

EARTH

TRANSLUNAR INJECTION

RENDEZVOUS AND DOCKING WITH COMMAND MODULE

MOON

TRANSEARTH INJECTION

Moon landing and exploration of Sea of Tranquility

Liftoff from Moon

PARKING ORBIT

Splashdown and recovery

Liftoff from Cape Canaveral

Lunar module descent

LUNAR ORBIT

RETURN TRIP TO EARTH

REENTRY INTO EARTH'S ATMOSPHERE

LUNAR ORBIT INSERTION

PARKING ORBIT

Neil Armstrong
1930 —

Neil Armstrong was born in Wapakoneta, Ohio, in 1930. When he was twelve years old, the Germans fired the first rocket into space. By 1958, the existing organization behind the American space program, the National Advisory Committee for Aeronauts (NACA), was replaced with the National Aeronautics and Space Administration (NASA). In 1959, NASA announced the names of the seven men they had selected to become the first astronauts, and the United States became a competitor to reach outer space.

Armstrong had a classic American boyhood. He was a Boy Scout, an avid reader, and a model-airplane enthusiast, and he worked making doughnuts for the local bakery. Armstrong had his first taste of flight at the age of six, when his father and he were passengers on an airplane. Ten years later, sixteen-year-old Armstrong earned his student pilot's license.

In order to gain further schooling as a pilot, Armstrong won a scholarship from the navy and enrolled in Purdue University. But the Korean War interrupted Armstrong's education. In 1950, Armstrong and his unit, Fighter Squadron 51, received orders to go to Korea. He completed his tour and returned to Purdue in 1952, where he met Janet

Shearon, who would become his wife.

After graduating from Purdue in 1955, Armstrong began working as a research pilot in the most technologically advanced aircraft in existence. Some of the flights took Armstrong over two hundred thousand feet up, higher than the earth's atmosphere. When the Mercury space program was being developed, Armstrong performed tests to help perfect a parachute system for the spacecraft's reentry. These tests were Armstrong's first steps toward becoming an astronaut.

In 1966, Armstrong became part of NASA's Gemini program. Gemini was the follow-up to the Mercury program, in which astronaut John Glenn became the first American to orbit the earth. NASA's ultimate

Neil Armstrong, Michael Collins, and Buzz Aldrin

The launch of *Apollo 11*, with astronauts Neil Armstrong, Michael Collins, and Buzz Aldrin, was scheduled for 9:32 a.m., July 16, 1969. In addition to the exhaustive checks and rechecks performed on every aspect of the spacecraft, the three astronauts had to pass a final test as well. Any sign of illness, even a stuffy nose, would be enough to ground the astronaut and postpone the mission. But Armstrong, Collins, and Aldrin were all completely healthy, and by six in the morning, they were getting into their flight suits.

In addition to their official equipment and provisions, each of the three astronauts carried several personal items, mementos that would be carried all the way to the moon and back. Armstrong's kit contained several miniature American flags and medals and a tape of some music Armstrong planned to play once on the moon over the radio for his wife.

By 7:52 a.m., the three astronauts were in place and the hatch had been closed. *Apollo 11* lifted off precisely on schedule. Approximately ten minutes after the launch, *Apollo 11* was in orbit 103 miles over the earth's surface. The component of the spacecraft carrying the thrust engine, called the SII, had already detached and dropped away as scheduled. Eventually the only components that would remain would be the command module, the service module (*Columbia*), and the lunar module (*Eagle*).

Three days after launching, *Apollo 11* was orbiting the moon. The following day, Neil Armstrong and Buzz Aldrin took their places in the lunar module, and *Eagle* and *Columbia* separated. While Collins continued to orbit the moon in *Columbia*, *Eagle* began its descent toward the area of the moon now called the Sea of Tranquility. At 4:18 p.m. on

goal was to place a man on the moon, and the Gemini missions were intended to help astronauts develop the skills and test the technologies required to accomplish this. The first *Gemini* was launched with the *Titan IV* rocket on June 3, 1965, and the missions continued every several months. The fifth Gemini mission, with the rocket *Titan VIII*, was scheduled for March 16, 1966. In command was Neil Armstrong, and piloting the controls was air force flier David Scott.

One of the main objectives of the Gemini–Titan VIII mission was for the astronauts to successfully dock the *Gemini* capsule to a separately launched and unmanned Agena rocket while in orbit. A lunar landing would involve the separation of the command module from the rocket for the surface touchdown, and the capsule would have to be redocked with the rocket in order to return to the earth. Armstrong and Scott rendezvoused with the Agena rocket and achieved a flawless docking. Their triumph was followed by a near disaster after undocking, when *Gemini* began spinning uncontrollably due to a faulty thruster. Though violently dizzy from the motion of the rotating craft, Armstrong and Scott used the reentry control system to guide the capsule back into the atmosphere for a successful splashdown.

July 20, the lunar module touched down safely. Six hours later, cocooned in his space suit and backpack called a portable life system, Neil Armstrong descended from *Eagle*'s ladder and took his first steps, uttering the now-famous statement, "That's one small step for man, one giant leap for mankind."

Aldrin soon followed, and the two astronauts spent the next two and a half hours collecting dust and rock samples from the moon's surface. They planted the American flag firmly in the surface and left several items behind, including a plaque inscribed: *Here men from the planet earth first set foot upon the moon. July 1969 AD. We came in peace for all mankind.* Before returning to

Eagle, Armstrong and Aldrin spoke with President Nixon over their radio.

After liftoff of the lunar module, *Eagle* and *Columbia* rendezvoused and docked, and the two spaceship components were one again. Two and a half days later, *Apollo 11* splashed down in the Pacific Ocean, and the United States celebrated with a parade.

Neil Armstrong, who won the Medal of Freedom for his work on *Apollo 11*, retired from NASA in 1971. For the next nine years, he taught aerospace engineering and later headed several technology-related companies before retiring. He has earned a permanent place in the ranks of history as a small-town boy who became the first man on the moon.

John Glenn

With the successful Soviet mission to orbit the earth in April 1961, NASA's desire to place an American into orbit became urgent. The astronaut chosen for the mission was John Glenn. Born in 1921 in Cambridge, Ohio, and raised during the Depression of the 1930s, Glenn became a marine fighter pilot who fought in both World War II and the Korean War. He had a heroic service record and a deep sense of patriotism, and was a ruggedly handsome family man. NASA would have been hard-pressed to find a more suitable hero for their space program.

Despite numerous delays, Glenn did eventually have a successful launch in the capsule *Friendship 7*, on February 20, 1962. He achieved orbit and circled the earth three times. The first American manned orbit of the earth delivered a huge shot of pride into the arm of the United States,

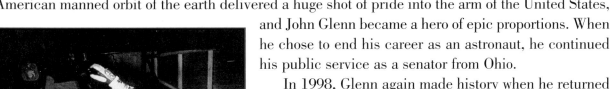

and John Glenn became a hero of epic proportions. When he chose to end his career as an astronaut, he continued his public service as a senator from Ohio.

In 1998, Glenn again made history when he returned to space aboard the shuttle *Discovery*. His presence on that mission allowed scientists to study the effects of space on aging and proved that older astronauts could tolerate the physical stress of space flight. Glenn's final space flight at the age of seventy-seven only confirmed what the world already knew—that he is an extraordinary man with infinite capabilities.

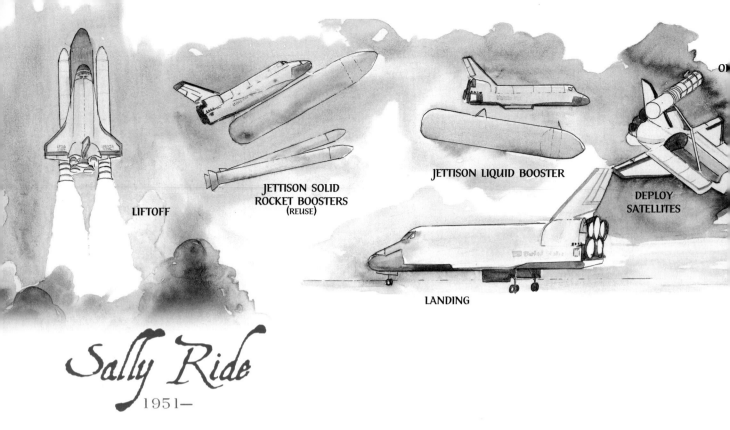

LIFTOFF

JETTISON SOLID
ROCKET BOOSTERS
(REUSE)

JETTISON LIQUID BOOSTER

DEPLOY
SATELLITES

LANDING

Sally Ride
1951–

Sally Ride did not spend her childhood dreaming of flying or reaching the moon or Mars. Ride was born in 1951, in Los Angeles, California. She was an athletic, intelligent, and confident girl, and all options seemed open to her. By the time she graduated from Los Angeles's Westlake High School, she had become such a good tennis player that a future as a tennis pro was a real possibility.

Ride attended Stanford University, where she studied physics and X-ray astronomy. She then obtained a doctoral degree in physics in 1978. While a student at Stanford, Ride saw a newspaper article announcing NASA was seeking scientists interested in training to become astronauts. Ride sent in her application, the first step in a long process that included interviews and tests to narrow down the over eight thousand interested candidates. Of the finalists, thirty-five were chosen to become astronauts, and six of those were women.

Though the Russians had long since put a woman into space, the United States had not yet achieved the same accomplishment. In the early 1960s, thirteen women fought the system and did everything possible to be included in the nation's space program. Though the women passed many of the most difficult tests given to male astronauts, their inclusion was nonetheless opposed on virtually all levels at NASA. The Mercury program and every other NASA space program until the space shuttle would remain exclusively the domain of male astronauts.

When Sally Ride was chosen to become an astronaut in 1978, the manned missions to the moon had ended. The next generation of space exploration would take place in the space shuttle. The shuttle program was different in many ways from the Apollo missions. For one, the space shuttle was designed to be reusable, like an airplane. It would transport astronauts into space, but instead of shedding components, the shuttle would land with all its parts intact. After some work, it would be ready for another flight.

The shuttle was also designed to be a work craft. It had a cargo bay, and it would be able to transport satellites into orbit and remove or repair malfunctioning satellites already there. NASA's purpose in seeking out scientists such as Sally Ride to train for shuttle missions was to create a group of "mission specialists" who could focus on experimental and repair activities, while the more traditional pilot-astronauts would take care of flying the space plane.

Ride spent most of 1978 and 1979 training, after which she had completed the eligibility requirements to be assigned to a shuttle mission. It was the seventh shuttle flight, called STS-7, to which Ride was assigned as a mission specialist and astronaut in 1983. The inclusion of a woman in the five-astronaut crew of STS-7 was national news. Though Ride insisted that she had entered the space program for the chance to fly in space, not to be the first woman to do so, the media storm was nonetheless intense. Ride was making American history, and the press wanted to know everything about her, including such peculiar details as whether she would be taking any lipstick or perfume along with her for the flight.

STS-7 was the second flight of the shuttle *Challenger*. The first five shuttle flights had been in the *Discovery*. STS-7's launch took place at the Kennedy Space Center in Florida on June 18, 1983. *Challenger* entered orbit at a height of approximately two hundred miles over the earth, and the shuttle completed one entire orbit every hour and a half. During the six days that *Challenger* spent in orbit, Ride and the other astronauts functioned in a completely weightless environment. They learned to work, eat, sleep, and socialize while floating.

Ride and the crew launched two commu-

Sally Ride on the flight deck

nications satellites from *Challenger*'s cargo bay and also performed a first-time exercise wherein a shuttle pallet satellite (SPAS) was released from *Challenger* to perform experiments and take photographs and then retrieved back on board the shuttle for return to earth. Among other functions, the SPAS took photographs of *Challenger*, providing the first pictures of a space shuttle in orbit.

Challenger landed at Edwards Air Force Base in California on June 24, 1983. Ride, now the first American woman in space, was the most sought-after female in the country. She turned down the many offers from Hollywood, explaining she had not entered the space program to make money or become a celebrity.

Ride continued her work with NASA, heading into space again in 1984 as a mission specialist on STS-41G, during which Kathryn Sullivan became the first American woman to walk in space. Ride received her next assignment as a mission specialist for

STS-61M. But she resigned from the mission in January 1986 after STS-51L resulted in the explosion of the shuttle *Challenger* and the loss of all seven of the crew on board. Rather than continue to train for the shuttle mission, Ride chose to join the Presidential Commission on the Space Shuttle Challenger Accident to investigate the tragedy's cause.

Ride left NASA in 1987 to begin a two-year fellowship at Stanford's Center for International Security and Arms Control. Several years later she returned to the academic world, becoming a professor of physics at the University of California at San Diego.

She also became an author, publishing several books about space. Always busy, she served as the director of the California Space Institute and founded Imaginary Lines, a company devoted to encouraging girls to pursue education and careers in the fields of science, math, and engineering.

Sally Ride will always be remembered as the first American woman in space, but she will also be remembered for her tireless work for the space program, for her students, and for her efforts to increase the number of females in many of the male-dominated fields of science.

Challenger's Last Flight

The shuttle *Challenger*, on which Sally Ride made both her space flights, later tragically achieved fame as the first American spacecraft to be lost during a manned mission. On January 28, 1986, the shuttle mission STS-51L launched from Cape Canaveral carrying three pilots, three scientists, and

a teacher. Christa McAuliffe was to become the first civilian in space. Seventy-three seconds after liftoff, a gas leak caused a fuel tank to rupture, and the resulting explosion broke *Challenger* apart. There were no survivors.

The accident stunned the country. It was the first time any American astronauts had been killed on duty since *Apollo 1*. It would take years for the investigation to expose all the system flaws that had contributed to the accident. The resulting changes in the design and to the system of launch approval were intended to reduce the chance that such an accident could occur again. Unfortunately, sixteen years later, the shuttle *Columbia* broke up over Texas during reentry. The accident reaffirmed that space travel, no matter how painstakingly monitored and regulated, will never be an entirely safe venture.

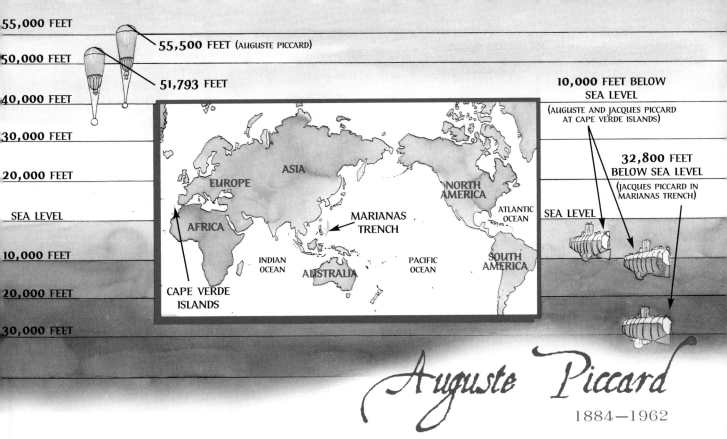

55,000 FEET

55,500 FEET (AUGUSTE PICCARD)

50,000 FEET

51,793 FEET

40,000 FEET

30,000 FEET

20,000 FEET

SEA LEVEL

10,000 FEET

20,000 FEET

30,000 FEET

10,000 FEET BELOW
SEA LEVEL

(AUGUSTE AND JACQUES PICCARD
AT CAPE VERDE ISLANDS)

32,800 FEET
BELOW SEA LEVEL

(JACQUES PICCARD IN
MARIANAS TRENCH)

SEA LEVEL

EUROPE
ASIA
AFRICA
NORTH
AMERICA
ATLANTIC
OCEAN
MARIANAS
TRENCH
INDIAN
OCEAN
AUSTRALIA
PACIFIC
OCEAN
SOUTH
AMERICA
CAPE VERDE
ISLANDS

Auguste Piccard

1884–1962

In 1884, when Auguste Piccard was born, the earth's stratosphere and the depths of the ocean must have seemed equally out of reach. Piccard and his twin brother, Jean, were born in Switzerland, sons of a physics professor at the University of Basel. From an early age, Piccard and his brother were surrounded by books. Like many other future oceanographers, Piccard became a great fan of Jules Verne's <u>Twenty Thousand Leagues Under the Sea</u>, published in 1870.

Auguste Piccard was nineteen when the Wright brothers made the historic first flight, from Kitty Hawk in December 1903. This first successful flight in a motor-powered airplane suspended all rules about what was possible. Piccard attended the Federal Poly-technic School of Switzerland, in Zurich, studying physics and engineering. Both he and his twin brother had learned to pilot bal-loons. While Jean married and moved to the United States to teach, Auguste began to meld his interest in ballooning with his study of physics and engineering. Piccard was a member of the Swiss Aero Club, dedicated to racing manned balloons across the ocean. At the time, no balloon could ascend as high as

the stratosphere, the frigid layer of the earth's atmosphere where there is not enough oxygen to breathe. But Piccard was convinced that he could design an airtight, pressurized cabin in which a balloonist could safely reach the stratosphere.

Though it was generally believed to be impossible, Piccard proved his doubters wrong on May 27, 1931. In his self-designed pressurized cabin, he climbed to 51,793 feet, becoming the first human to reach the strato-sphere. The following year, he set a new record, reaching 55,500 feet. Following this ascent, he is said to have promised his wife, the mother of his five children, to stop bal-looning into the stratosphere. Piccard already

117

Auguste Piccard in the cockpit of his gondola

had his attention focused elsewhere. He reasoned that if his pressurized cabin could safely carry a person to the deadly environment of the stratosphere, a similar version could be designed to carry him safely to the bottom of the sea.

At this time, the deepest sea dive on record had been made by American scientist William Beebe in 1934. Beebe had designed a bathysphere, or "deep ball," which was a steel chamber supplied with a flow of oxygen through a cable. The bathysphere was lowered by the cable to the ocean floor by a ship on the surface. On his 1934 dive, Beebe reached a depth of 3,028 feet, over half a mile. Piccard applauded this accomplishment but believed his pressurized bathyscaphe, or "deep boat," could go even deeper without relying on a cable, which could easily snap.

The greatest problem facing Piccard was how to design a system that would first go to the ocean floor, then rise back to the surface. He devised a combination of ballast to weigh down the bathyscaphe and flotation devices to lift it. The system consisted of iron pellets and detachable floats filled with gasoline, which is lighter than water. The iron pellets

would act as a weight to carry the craft to the ocean floor. The pellets would then be released, and the floats of gasoline would cause the bathyscaphe to rise to the surface.

To make his portholes, Piccard used two layers of the newly invented material Plexiglas, which is transparent and flexible enough to bend slightly under water pressure without shattering. The pressure of the water was always a serious consideration—the deeper the dive, the stronger the pressure. At the deepest-known area of the ocean floor, approximately thirty-five thousand feet, a human being without protection would be instantly crushed to death. Just like Beebe before him, Piccard knew that the sphere shape of his bathyscaphe would distribute the intense pressure of the water equally so that it would not collapse.

Piccard did not want to risk anyone's life, so he planned the first deep dive to be unmanned. The dive was scheduled to take place in October 1948, off the western coast of Africa, near the Cape Verde Islands. The vessel would be rigged with an automatic switch that would release the iron ballast as soon as the sphere touched down. Before the deep-water dive took place, Piccard and his Belgian partner, Max Cosyns, tested the bathyscaphe on a relatively short dive of only seventy-four feet. After the systems checked out accurately on the test dive, the bathyscaphe was prepared for its unmanned descent to over four thousand feet. Piccard intended to follow up the first deep-water dive with a second, manned descent. However, when the unmanned bathyscaphe resurfaced, the seas had become extremely rough. The support ship could not lift Piccard's vessel back on board because the floats of gasoline it carried made it too dangerous under the conditions. Piccard decided that his only choice was to jettison the floats of gasoline—his only supply—putting an end to the plans for a manned dive.

Piccard was never one to be discouraged by failure. Assisted by his son, Jacques, he designed a new bathyscaphe that could be towed to its dive spot rather than having to rely on a support vessel to lift it in and out of the water. The new bathyscaphe was named *Trieste,* after the Italian hometown of the industrialists who had donated money to finance the new vessel. In 1953, father and son set a new depth record in the *Trieste,* descending to a depth of over ten thousand feet. Auguste Piccard had the unique distinction of having been higher in the sky and lower in the sea than any other human being before him.

In 1954, the seventy-year-old Piccard decided to retire from diving. He did not stop working, however, and remained determined to send a human to the deepest reaches of the ocean. His son, Jacques, was ready to lead the way.

Jacques Piccard

Jacques Piccard shared his father's goal of reaching the very deepest area known to exist in the ocean, the Marianas Trench. It is a canyon so huge, it could conceal all of Mount Everest with an additional mile to spare. The bottom is over thirty-six thousand feet down, more than four miles deeper than the Piccards' previous record-breaking dive. The trench is two hundred miles off the coast of Guam, in the Pacific Ocean. On January 23, 1960, Jacques Piccard and U.S. Navy Lieutenant Donald Walsh boarded the *Trieste* and prepared to descend.

The controlled descent to the ocean floor took nearly five hours. They rested on the bottom only long enough to switch on their searchlight and see a fish, proof that life could exist at that bone-crushing depth. Carrying forward with his father's dream, Jacques Piccard had reached a depth of 35,800 feet, 6.78 miles straight down. In doing so, father and son opened the door to the last great unexplored frontier on earth.

Jacques Piccard and Andreas Rechnitzer on the USN bathyscaphe *Trieste*

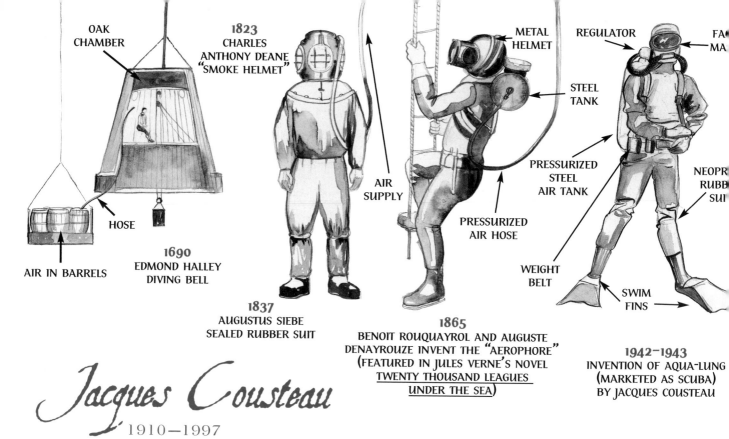

OAK CHAMBER

HOSE

AIR IN BARRELS

1690
EDMOND HALLEY
DIVING BELL

1823
CHARLES ANTHONY DEANE
"SMOKE HELMET"

AIR SUPPLY

1837
AUGUSTUS SIEBE
SEALED RUBBER SUIT

METAL HELMET

STEEL TANK

PRESSURIZED STEEL AIR TANK

PRESSURIZED AIR HOSE

WEIGHT BELT

1865
BENOIT ROUQUAYROL AND AUGUSTE
DENAYROUZE INVENT THE "AEROPHORE"
(FEATURED IN JULES VERNE'S NOVEL
TWENTY THOUSAND LEAGUES
UNDER THE SEA)

REGULATOR

FA... MA...

NEOPR... RUBB... SUI...

SWIM FINS

1942–1943
INVENTION OF AQUA-LUNG
(MARKETED AS SCUBA)
BY JACQUES COUSTEAU

Jacques Cousteau
1910–1997

Jacques Cousteau was born in France in 1910. As a boy, he was small and sickly, an unlikely constitution for a future diver and oceanographer. But he always felt a magical attraction to water, dreaming of touching it and immersing himself in it.

Jacques, his mother, and his brother, Pierre, traveled frequently with Jacques' father, who worked for an American millionaire. In addition to his love of water, Cousteau also displayed an early interest in mechanical things, particularly movie cameras. He could take one apart and accurately put it back together with little effort. Perhaps searching for a way to combine his fascination with the sea with his interest in mechanics, Cousteau entered the French naval academy in 1930. He intended to study aviation, but his plans were interrupted by a devastating car accident, after which doctors came very close to amputating one of his arms.

During the slow road to recovery, Cousteau began to swim each day to regain strength. But he would never be strong enough to qualify for the navy's aviation school. Instead, Cousteau was stationed at a base in Toulon as an artillery instructor. While at Toulon, he continued his daily swims and met fellow water enthusiasts Philippe Tailliez and Frederic Dumas. The trio free-dove together, frequently going down as far as thirty feet. It was during this time that Cousteau and his friends began experimenting with makeshift diving equipment. Cousteau first obtained a pair of aviator goggles and modified them to be airtight. The resulting dive literally opened an entirely new world. For the first time, Cousteau could clearly see the abundant life and beauty that flourished beneath the ocean's surface. Now that he could see underwater, he wanted more time to dive than between breaths. He began to focus on a system that would allow him to carry his own oxygen with him during dives.

The technology to compress air into a canister already existed. The challenge to Cousteau was to find a way for a diver to have access to that air when needed and to stop the flow between breaths. Engineer Emil Gagnan already knew of a valve designed to conserve gas. When Cousteau saw it in 1942, he immediately adapted it to regulate oxygen, and his diving invention called Aqua-Lung was born.

With this idea, now called scuba (for self-contained underwater breathing apparatus), Cousteau single-handedly invented diving as we know it. He began with Tailliez and Dumas to explore the limits of diving. To do so, they had to risk their own lives. In experimenting with how deep a human could safely dive, Cousteau discovered and named the "rapture of the deep" syndrome, in which nitrogen released into the blood by the water's pressure causes the diver to become disoriented and confused, often leading to death by drowning. In 1956, Cousteau's fellow diver Maurice Fargues died of this syndrome after reaching a 396-foot depth. Thereafter, Cousteau set his limit for diving at three hundred feet.

By the late 1940s, Aqua-Lung was available for sale commercially. Cousteau was already looking ahead to the next phase of his career. He had founded the Undersea Research Group for the navy, which experimented with both diving and underwater photography. But Cousteau wanted to expand. He found financial backing to purchase an old minesweeper and converted it to a research vessel called *Calypso* with a diving well and observation chamber. In 1952, he received funding from the National Geographic Society to undertake several new missions. The following year, he wrote a successful book about his experiences titled *The Silent World*.

Cousteau had already made several films about his diving, and in 1956, he made a documentary film version of *The Silent World*. The film was an extraordinary success, winning the Cannes Film Festival's highest award and taking an Oscar in the United States. Jacques Cousteau was famous, and the world had its first glimpse of life beneath the sea.

Cousteau's next project was to allow humans to spend more time underwater. He built a sea station, called Conshelf, designed to house two divers, who could live there for a week and use the station both as living quarters and as the base for dives. The station was followed by Conshelf II and later Conshelf III in 1965. Cousteau's son Philippe was one of the aquanauts who spent a month living at 330 feet below the ocean surface.

For the next nine years, Cousteau devoted much of his time to filming a television series called *The Undersea World of Jacques Cousteau*. Now a household name, Cousteau spent increasing amounts of time educating his viewers about how much damage we had already inflicted on the ocean and the importance of changing our ways in order to protect marine life. He founded Cousteau Society in

Jacques Cousteau emerges from a submarine.

1974 to pursue marine conservation and to discourage further pollution of the ocean.

By the late 1970s, a new generation of nature documentaries competed with Cousteau's, and he began making fewer television programs. The death of his son Philippe in a seaplane accident in 1979 was a serious blow. Cousteau continued his work on behalf of the oceans and undersea life despite other personal difficulties, including the death of his wife of fifty years in 1990.

Cousteau remarried and kept working through the first half of the decade. In 1996, his beloved boat *Calypso* sank after a collision with a barge. He immediately began making plans for *Calypso II,* but in June 1997, he died of heart and respiratory failure at the age of eighty-seven. Until the end of his life he was planning ahead for the future, with his hopes and dreams resting, as always, in the sea.

Diving Before Aqua-Lung

For centuries before Jacques Cousteau was born, people made deep dives to hunt for valuable items such as pearls or sponges. Using no equipment, divers were always limited by the amount of air they could hold in their lungs and the amount of water pressure they could withstand.

One of the earliest inventions designed to get people underwater for longer than a single breath was a diving bell, which took barrels of air down with it and could remain submerged for over an hour. The year was 1690 and the inventor was Edmond Halley, better known for the comet that bears his name.

In 1837, the world's first helmeted diving suit appeared on the scene. But the suit, attached by an oxygen hose to the surface, was heavy and clumsy. The next major innovation in deep-sea exploration did not occur until 1930, when American William Beebe created his huge, ball-shaped bathysphere, which could carry two people almost fifteen hundred feet down. But the bathysphere could only dangle like a yo-yo at the end of a cable. To water lovers such as Jacques Cousteau, nothing could replace the experience of diving down into the water itself. Yves le Prieur took another step toward giving divers this freedom when he invented a pressurized air tank in 1933, but the tank had to be opened manually for each breath. By the time Aqua-Lung was invented, the world had been waiting for centuries to reach the bottom of the sea.

William Beebe and Otis Barton pose with their invention, the bathysphere.

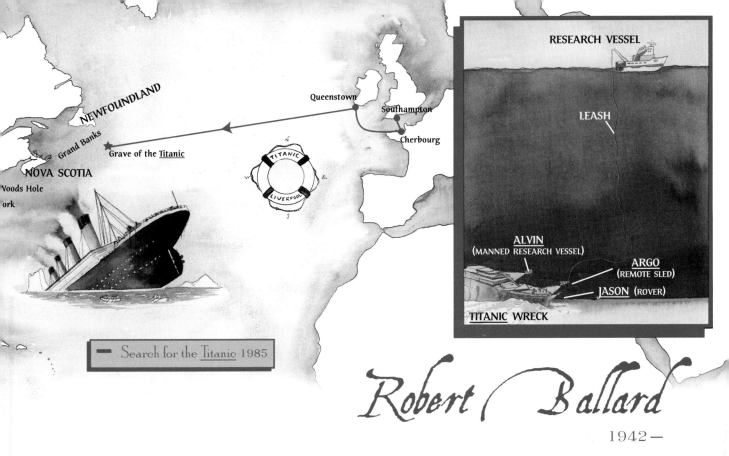

Search for the Titanic 1985

Robert Ballard

1942–

Robert Ballard, the man who would become famous for exploring the deepest reaches of the ocean, was born in Wichita, Kansas, where you could go hundreds of miles in any direction without finding the sea. But when his family moved to San Diego, California, the sea became a part of Ballard's life. From childhood, the ocean and all that lay beneath its surface fascinated him. After reading Jules Verne's Twenty Thousand Leagues Under the Sea, he became particularly interested in submarines. Ballard studied oceanography at the University of Hawaii, working as a dolphin trainer in his spare hours. On completing graduate school, he worked at North American Aviation in the Ocean Systems Group, developing underwater research missions.

During the Vietnam War, Ballard served with the Office of Naval Research, and part of his job was to work as the liaison to the Woods Hole Oceanographic Institution in Massachusetts, one of the country's most famous centers for ocean study. He would work there for the next thirty years, and it was at WHOI that Ballard had his first exposure to diving submersibles. WHOI had its own diving submersible, called *Alvin*, still one of the world's most famous deep-diving research submersibles. Ballard had his first chance to join a dive on *Alvin* in July 1972, to retrieve geological samples from the ocean bottom. The dive convinced Ballard of what he already suspected—submersibles such as *Alvin* were more than vehicles for exploration. They were the most important tool for underwater research in the history of ocean study.

Ballard participated in the 1972 French-American expedition to map the Mid-Atlantic Ridge—a ridge and valley comparable in size

Robert Ballard during a 1987 book tour

Using extensive data to calculate the site of the sinking, including *Titanic*'s last known coordinates and areas already searched by the French, *Argo* scanned the ocean bottom with its cameras. But day after day it turned up nothing.

Just five days before the scheduled end of the mission, a team member who was constantly watching the monitor that displayed *Argo*'s images saw something on the ocean floor that he thought looked like a boiler. When the tape was played back and compared to photographs of *Titanic,* it was all but certain that the object seen was one of *Titanic*'s huge boilers. Ballard and his team had found the debris trail that would lead them to the lost ocean liner.

The following day, *Argo* was sending up pictures of the ship itself. The pictures were haunting images of the massive ocean liner and the scattered remains of objects it had once carried. When Ballard arrived home with the news and the images, he was an instant celebrity. He returned the following year with *Alvin* and *Jason Junior,* a remotely operated camera that Ballard called the swimming eyeball. This time Ballard's camera was able to enter the ship itself, capturing extraordinary pictures of the ship's interior, some of its luxurious features still completely intact.

In 1989, Ballard established the Jason Project in response to the overwhelming interest schoolchildren expressed in the story of how *Titanic* was found. The project used Ballard's remote-operated camera-bearing vehicle, *Jason,* to broadcast exploration programs to students throughout the United States and Canada, allowing them to watch as events unfolded. When *Jason* located and recorded images of the Roman ship *Isis,* wrecked some two thousand years earlier, the broadcast of the discovery was seen by a huge audience of students.

to the Grand Canyon but inaccessibly located at the bottom of the Atlantic Ocean. These and later dives brought back important new information on the makeup of the earth's crust and previously unknown species, many of which clustered around vents on the deep ocean floor that spout minerals and generate incredible heat.

For more than a decade, Ballard worked to raise funds for and interest in *Alvin,* using the submersible for underwater research and ultimately to fulfill one of his long-held dreams: to locate the wreck of the RMS *Titanic.* He also began to develop his own technology, called the Argo/Jason system, which would use two connected vehicles operated by remote control. The smaller vehicle would be a highly maneuverable sledge carrying a video camera that would transmit images to the remote operator on the surface.

With *Argo* ready and *Alvin* available for deep diving until *Jason* was completed, Ballard got his chance to go after *Titanic.* In partnership with a French institution, the expedition began in July 1985. Ballard and his American team had only limited time with *Alvin* before the sub would have to return to Woods Hole for its next scheduled mission.

Ballard has continued to develop and use his robotic underwater technology to find or explore lost ships, such as the German battleship *Bismarck*, the *Lusitania*, the lost American fleet from the battle of Guadalcanal in World War II, and a fifteen-hundred-year-old shipwreck in the Black Sea. He retired from WHOI and became president of the Institute for Exploration at the Mystic Aquarium and Seaport in Connecticut. The institute, which Ballard also founded, is dedicated to the pursuit of underwater exploration, archaeology, and research and to developing new systems and vehicles capable of delving into ever more remote areas beneath the great oceans.

Ballard once said that the public knew more about Mars and Venus than about the deep sea. With the technology and dedication he has brought to undersea exploration, it is very likely that soon that statement will no longer be true.

Titanic

The tragedy of *Titanic* is one of the most famous of our times. The ocean liner RMS *Titanic* was designed to be the greatest and most luxurious ship in the world. She was commonly thought to be unsinkable. But on the night of April 14, 1912, the most magnificent of all oceangoing vessels became the most awe-inspiring shipwreck in history.

At 882 feet, nine inches in length, with a capacity for 3,547 crew and passengers, *Titanic* was the largest passenger vessel on earth. Its luxurious interior matched those of the most expensive hotels. Her passenger list included some of the wealthiest and most privileged people in society. When *Titanic* left England on her first voyage, on April 10, 1912, it was a grand event. Disaster struck four days later.

Just before midnight, *Titanic* collided with an iceberg, ripping open a section of her starboard bow. At first, it seemed to crew and passengers alike that the ocean liner would weather the blow. But within hours, the ship was clearly sinking. Tragically, *Titanic* carried enough lifeboats for barely half the passengers and crew on board. By the time the sun rose the next morning, there were approximately 710 survivors in lifeboats. More than fifteen hundred had lost their lives. The ship itself, resting at the bottom of the ocean, would remain undisturbed and unseen until seventy-three years later, when Robert Ballard and his team would first catch sight of a massive boiler lying on the ocean floor.

RMS *Titanic* in dock before journey

Index

** Page numbers in *italics* refer to illustrations.*